The
ZEN CIGAR SESSHIN

The
ZEN CIGAR SESSHIN

J. F. WESTBROOK

32565 Golden Lantern Ste. B #161
Dana Point, California 92629
Email: pppatdp@gmail.com

Library of Congress Cataloging-in-Publication Data available on file.
The Zen Cigar Sesshin / J. F. Westbrook

ISBN 978-1-7345184-0-5 (print)
ISBN 978-1-7345184-1-2 (EBook)

1. Zen Buddhism 2. Cigars 3. Spiritualism

For Ava Grace,
    my little Buddha.

CONTENTS

Prologue   xi

Preface   xiii

Introduction   xix

The Encounter   3

Sesshin Structure   19

Sesshin Starters   37

Establish Your Own ZCS   46

Prologue to Primers   48

Zen Primer   55

Cigar Primer   115

About the Author   183

"Wisdom is a quality of the psychological or spiritual relationship between man and his experience." - ALAN W. WATTS

PROLOGUE

We read and hear a lot about the ego, what it does, what it seeks and how it manipulates us to get what it wants and needs to survive, but not much about how it came to be. We know that we must lose it in order to get in touch with our true nature – our Being, but not really why it is so difficult to do so.

Humans evolved as animals and we continue to evolve. Some of us have become enlightened, moving beyond the purely animal state to where evolution will ultimately take all mankind if we don't self-destruct as a species before that happens. But before the ego, as animals we had our instinct with all that came with it, particularly our primal sense of self-preservation. The human sense of self-preservation had to be greater than that of the rest of the animals on the planet in order to put us at the top of the food chain. But while attaining that lofty position we gradually lost sight of our universal connection as our former animal instinct was gradually replaced with a solipsistic sense of self-worth, or ego. With our ability to constantly reflect on our accomplishments the ego only grew stronger as we continued to evolve. Clearly the next step in human evolution needs to be an attenuation of the ego in order to realize our inner Being. Not an easy endeavor but one that needs to take place to ensure our survival.

PREFACE

The idea of the Zen Cigar Sesshin (ZCS) developed over time following a chance encounter many years ago with a wonderful old Asian gentleman. A somewhat solitary individual, one could easily take him for a Zen master; there was certainly no doubt in recognizing him as a cigar aficionado. Periodically he would get together with a few close friends, all of whom were cigar smoking Zen practitioners. For an hour or so they would enjoy a fine cigar and discuss their Zen practice. I met this man during what I describe as the Encounter, and I was subsequently invited to sit with him and a couple of his friends for a smoke and a discussion. Afterwards, I thought about how liberating the experience was and how comfortable I felt with no distractions, discussing Zen and enjoying a fine cigar. Over time I began making notes based on the experience, and thinking of ways to build on the gentleman's "get together" to enhance one's Zen practice. In doing so I arrived at the concept of the Zen Cigar Sesshin and ultimately this book. The book itself is not meant to instruct, but rather as a guide to augment a particular facet of one's Zen practice.

The author is by no means a master or teacher of Zen, merely a practitioner and advocate, as well as a smoker of fine cigars. I have been practicing Zen for some years now and have been smoking cigars virtually all of my adult life. A primary reason I decided to write this book was to investigate the ego through focused, open discussions. Subsequent to attending a Zen Cigar Sesshin we may work individually to mitigate its influence as we recall our joint talks.

There was another strong motivation for the book. Although Zen would have us look inward for the truth, there are also Zen masters or Zen teachers who help to point the way for us. But Zen masters or teachers are not readily available in every city or suburb. Moreover, I am certain that beyond our individual practice many of us would like to attend and participate along with others at established Zen Centers or Zendos, Zen masters and teachers notwithstanding. Unfortunately, the Zen centers that do exist are not conveniently accessible to many. And certainly cigar smoking would be frowned upon, if not outright prohibited, at those that do exist; thus, the appeal of a local Zen Cigar Sesshin.

At a Zen Cigar Sesshin, groups of like-minded individuals are able to come together at their convenience and within their own geographic area to participate in a structured Zen event, while simultaneously incorporating a fine cigar in their experience. Doing so in a structured yet relaxed intimate collective, rather than individually, while enjoying a good cigar adds another dimension to our practice that can provide added benefit.

Cigars are a part of the Zen Cigar Sesshin for a few reasons, not the least of which is the calming effect they have on the smoker. Zen has been described as the calming of nervous energy. One would imagine, therefore, that the two pursuits would complement one another. Also, the time it takes to smoke a good cigar has been established as the nominal amount of time for the duration of a Zen Cigar Sesshin.

A further benefit of attending a Zen Cigar Sesshin is that the group can achieve a greater level of presence, more so than on an individual basis. Their collective participation raises the amount of presence of each person in the group when they have a focus on remaining mindful. It will be incumbent upon the Host to remain the beacon of mindfulness during a Zen Cigar Sesshin to maintain this collective consciousness – a serious responsibility.

We practice zazen to realize the One Body and our true nature, which may manifest with the loss of the ego and eventual enlightenment. During the Zen Cigar Sesshin we talk openly about the ego. This is done within a structure that reinforces a Zen approach, emphasizes a natural simplicity and allows us to explore ways to promote the compassion we obtain as a result of losing ourselves.

INTRODUCTION

The general focus of the Zen Cigar Sesshin is the ego, arguably the greatest impediment to experiencing life as it should truly be experienced – simply being and doing in the present moment. The Zen Cigar Sesshin is an exercise in the Zen tradition that employs exploratory discussions, shared experiences and observations about the ego's effect on us, and how to deal with it in order to improve our lives. Using fundamental Buddhist precepts as benchmarks we will investigate their validity, recognize their importance and determine how to continually practice and refine them as situations may require.

A "Sesshin" is a Zen retreat where attendees practice extended periods of zazen. The word is Japanese and is made from two words: "*setsu*" - touching and "*shin*" - mind. It is usually translated as "touching the mind." A typical Sesshin includes many participants and can go on for days, during which attendees may not communicate with one another except during intermittent breaks and evening meals. It is a time for intense introspection where one may achieve deep *Samadhi*, or concentration. During the Zen Cigar Sesshin the intention is still to touch the mind, but through interaction among a limited number of participants with meaningful communication through focused dialogue. The aim is to expand participants' awareness and understanding of the topics discussed.

When we forget our self, as Dogen

Sengi said, we mitigate our *dukkha*, or suffering. The word mitigate is appropriate because until we can truly live in the world of the Absolute and the Relative simultaneously through the sustained realization of both, suffering will continue to be an issue, wearing us down both mentally and physically as it undermines our happiness in the process. In fact, suffering will always be a part of our life, but with the absence of the ego it will be nothing special.

Zazen affords us the opportunity to realize the One Body and our true nature on an individual and deeply personal level. Koan practice requires a collaborative process between teacher and pupil to achieve the same result. Employing either or both methods strengthens our practice and helps us maintain our Zen way of life. The interactive discussions that occur during a Zen Cigar Sesshin combine traits of both zazen, with its single pointed concentration, and koans, which involve the pupil's intuitive thought process and subsequent response to a teacher. Additionally, the inclusion of the participants smoking cigars together during the Zen Cigar Sesshin is at once a personal and collective endeavor. Moreover, smoking cigars relaxes the participants while creating harmony among the group as a whole, allowing their discussions to be more candid and productive overall. While zazen is practiced daily and a single koan may take from weeks to years before the answer is intuitively realized, ideally Zen practitioners who also appreciate a good cigar will attend a Zen Cigar Sesshin on a regular basis to complement their Zen practice.

There are a number of issues paramount to Zen which must be realized in order to live life fully: the fact that nothing is permanent; the fact that there is no past or future, only the present moment; the fact that we are all part of the One Body and all have the Buddha Nature but do not realize it. Our ability to accept these truths require a deep understanding and acknowledgement on our part of how the ego works to prevent us from living life as it should be lived. The reason for investigating the ego during the Zen Cigar Sesshin is to identify and understand the deleterious effect it has at the individual as well as at the collective level based on Zen Buddhist teachings and precepts. A number of generic talking points (Sesshin Starters) have been included, but in time participants will most likely expand the list to include their own talking points.

Zen tells us that we are not who we think we are. We have all heard the saying "He is a legend in his own mind" to describe a person with an overly inflated ego. But the fact is that to varying degrees, everyone is guilty of this condition. It is the result of our attachment to our ideas, notions and concepts. We have come to believe that we are who we "think" we are rather than who we really are. We have come to be defined by our past actions, our future aspirations and our ideologies. As we attach to our ideas, concepts and notions we believe that we exist separate from others with whom we do not share the same physical attributes, place of origin, social standing, ideology or spiritual belief. All of this dualistic thinking creates our fear and is the work of the ego, which would have us believe we must constantly place our interests above those of everything and everyone else; otherwise we are somehow weak or even a failure. We can't just compete, we must to win. We can't just climb a mountain, we must conquer it!

Although humanity has made incredible strides and advancements in everything from science to government, the standard operating condition of most human minds could certainly be described as flawed. The flaw, of course, is the way in which the ego operates. It manifests in all areas of human advancement, from the development and use of things like weapons of mass destruction and political gridlock and intrigue to the slow death of the planet itself through a disregard for the environment that sustains all life on it. This modus operandi is obvious today, and it is spreading rapidly. Man's technological advances have aided in this mental flaw becoming a collective mind-set. We now interact globally through social media. And although its intent began as a way to make and stay in touch with friends, it is rapidly becoming something quite the contrary; a tool of empowerment for the darkest side of the ego.

If the world is going to be a better place to live in then we must make it so. Zen tells us that for the world to be a better place we as individuals must be better. It also tells us that we are already better because we have the Buddha Nature within us, but that we have lost sight of that fact. We do not, however, become better by simply trying to be good or better, we must first actually realize our true nature on an intuitive level. Then we must continue to work on that realization every day through our practice of zazen and mindfulness. Only then will there be a shift in our consciousness and through our subsequent actions a shift in a global consciousness. The Zen Cigar Sesshin is another activity along this path.

Practicing Zen stabilizes us by

strengthening our resolve in the One Body and our true nature. Zen reminds us that we are each at the same time unique and different in the Relative world of form, and that it is our differences that make us the same within the Absolute universe of emptiness. Although this is an irrefutable fact, we must each realize it for ourselves. The way to do this is to lose the ego. When we do we will awaken to the present moment and to our everyday life of enlightenment. This is the result of losing ourselves. When we lose ourselves we function in the Relative world without discrimination or dualistic thinking and acknowledge the Absolute, seeing things just as they are – nothing special.

The Zen Cigar Sesshin is a means to help us strengthen our Zen practice through an open discourse that will shed light on the solipsistic workings of the ego and at the same time help us to develop techniques to keep it in check. During a Zen Cigar Sesshin, we examine the ego and discuss how to recognize it, understand what it is, how it works and how to keep it in check. Ultimately, through practice and various techniques, there will be a shift in consciousness where one will be able to recognize his or her ego's attempt to manipulate a situation. People will then be able to quickly assess a situation and make a spontaneous and appropriate situational decision.

It is easy to view one's self as an individual apart from all others. Even easier, it would appear that as human beings we are separate from the animal and plant life that inhabits the earth. And as living beings we are obviously separate and apart from the inanimate environment, both natural and manmade. Yet Zen tells us that in reality we are inextricably linked to and a part of every other thing in the universe. Our difference as sentient beings is that we are aware of our existence. We can make decisions and act on them as a result of our ability to think, not merely react based on instinct alone.

Zen draws from Mahayana Buddhism and Chinese Taoism. It incorporates the

Tao philosophy, or the Way, which says that the universe is spontaneous and flows naturally, and that all things are perfect just as they are. It is a place for peaceful coexistence. For humans there should be tranquility and harmony among all. So how do we follow the Way and coexist peacefully within the Relative world – the world of form? We start by realizing the truth that we all have the Buddha Nature – our true nature. Over the millennia we have lost sight of this and must realize it through a shift in consciousness, which may occur during our practice. It is during this journey toward awakening that we begin to realize the truth and significance of the One Body. And although Zen is not a science, a popular scientific theory may help put this realization in perspective.

Consider the Big Bang Theory. It postulates that billions of years ago nothing existed. Then from something the size of the tip of a pin, a massive explosion erupted from which emanated all matter that comprises the universe. The explosion occurred with such power and force that all matter continues to expand outward to this day, with no sign of ceasing. Over time that matter coalesced and changed, and the changes continue. One of the results of those changes is the existence of human beings, comprised of elements of matter common throughout the entire universe. While different as individuals, each human being is "universally" the same, no better or worse than anyone or anything else in the universe. This is why Zen tells us to treat all things with the same reverence and regard; and why when an angry child slams a door a wise parent will say "Why did you slam the door? What did it ever do to you?" The child doesn't know it but the answer, of course, is the ego.

Humans are continually thinking. The stream of consciousness, as it were, continues to revisit past events and to link those thoughts in such a way as to build on them so that ultimately we come to believe that we are who we are based on those collective thoughts. This, however, is the illusion. We construct an internal narrative that we come to rely on as our own reality from which we base current and future decisions and actions. When we are able to catch ourselves and observe this internal thought process we reveal our true nature, if only briefly. For at that moment we are living in the present as part of the One Body. This is the big mind observing the workings of the small mind; the big "I" watching the little "I". As we develop our Zen practice we are able to extend these moments, which helps give us the ability to act spontaneously, without discrimination or dualistic thinking based on attachments to preconceived thoughts or notions. This is not to say that thoughts, notions, ideas or concepts are bad things; we all need them to function in the Relative world. But when we attach to them they cause our *dukkha*, our suffering. So we may use them, just not be used by them.

As we continue our practice we may awaken and experience full Enlightenment or we may not. Either way, to some degree we will experience a shift in our consciousness that will allow us to recognize the thinker for what it is - the ego that wants to be in control. Of course, the only thing we can control is our own actions. When our practice is strong we will realize and accept this with more frequency. We then begin to live our life in the present within the realm of the Absolute and the Relative simultaneously. When we do this our actions project an optimistic sentiment that when noticed by others as something positive fosters emulation. The Zen Cigar Sesshin is but another way to continue our practice.

The book begins with the Encounter, a narrative of the precipitous dream of an event that over time I developed to become the Zen Cigar Sesshin. Following this is the Structure for the Zen Cigar Sesshin itself. This section includes an outline of the formal organization and protocol for conducting and attending a Zen Cigar Sesshin. It involves a participant's actions prior to and during a Zen Cigar Sesshin. It includes the roles of those in attendance, how the participants are to comport themselves and the significance of that comportment. The guidelines foster a productive meeting and reinforcement of Zen principles and practices for addressing the ego. Next, the Sesshin Starters section is based on and includes thoughts regarding Buddhist precepts relevant to the ego. Each Sesshin will begin with a hypothetical or actual situational example of the ego at work. The Sesshin Starters are provided to aid in beginning a discussion when necessary. Whether used to spark a particular situation or addressed in the broad sense as listed, they are there to maintain focus on the ego as the topic of the discussions. The final section of the book includes a Zen Primer and a Cigar Primer, preceded by their Prologue. These are very brief overviews of the two subjects at hand, intended only to familiarize a participant with the history of each should that be necessary. Both have been around for more than two-thousand years in one form or another, and both should be appreciated in their own right.

The
ZEN CIGAR SESSHIN

THE ENCOUNTER

One morning some time ago I met a gray-haired Asian fellow at the conclusion of one of my business trips. I was staying at a hotel by the water in a small coastal town. The hotel was 'U'-shaped, with a pool in the center and lush landscaping throughout the grounds. There was an inviting outdoor lanai facing the ocean just off the center of the building, which is where I encountered the gentleman. He was sitting alone at a small table under a large blue umbrella on that brilliant day. I could not help but notice that he was reading a large book about Zen Buddhism. Never the introvert, I approached the man.

"I see you're reading about Zen," I said.

The man looked up and nodded his head once in agreement.

"I've been into Zen for a while now." I said.

"Is that so," he said.

"Yes," I said. "Though it's funny, you know, how it seems so straightforward but is so hard to practice."

"Umm, the Western mind, I believe, requires more time," he said.

"Possibly," I said, and introduced myself.

"I am Toshi," he said.

"My pleasure, Toshi," I said.

"Are you vacationing?" Toshi said. "This is a lovely place for vacationing."

"No, I was here on business."

"Ah."

"And you," I said.

"I live in town. This is a peaceful place, and I enjoy a cup of tea here after my tai chi."

Toshi was so peaceful; the way he sat, the way he spoke, even the way he closed the book when I approached. I had never before encountered such serenity in an individual.

"You say you *were* here on business, yet you are still here," Toshi said.

"Actually, I wrapped up my business a bit sooner than expected last night. I have an 11:00 a.m. flight out tomorrow, but it's such a great day I've decided not to reschedule for an earlier flight. Thought I would just take the day and explore the town a bit. Which reminds me; you wouldn't happen to know where I can buy a quality cigar, would you? I thought I might enjoy one this evening after dinner."

Toshi cocked his head slightly and looked at me. "So, you appreciate a good cigar?" he said.

"I do," I said. "Particularly on a day like today, and in a place like this."

"And you are a student of Zen," Toshi said.

"Well, I try. I've been reading about it a few years, and have attended dharma talks at a Zen center. I try to live mindfully but it's challenging. Some things seem clear, yet comprehending something like non-duality is difficult," I said.

At this Toshi invited me to sit at his table.

As I sat across the table from Toshi under the blue umbrella, he leaned forward almost imperceptibly and asked if I practiced my zazen. I told him I did and he asked if I did it daily. I told him that I tried, and that I prefer early morning, conditions permitting. But it was not always possible. He gave a slight sigh and told me that for most, zazen is the way to awakening.

"Enlightenment," I said.

"It has many names," he said,

"enlightenment, satori, awakening, nirvana, kensho and others. It is the realization of your true Being, your Buddha spirit. And for this, continued practice of zazen is most helpful."

"Can enlightenment come without zazen?"

"Enlightenment may never come, with or without meditation. Many experience satori without ever sitting in the crossed-leg position. Either way you must continue your practice after your awakening, and zazen is most beneficial for your practice."

"So, zazen is the heart of Zen practice?" I said.

"I would say that the core is to live mindfully, just being and doing, accepting life as it presents itself to you," Toshi said.

"You know, I could sit here talking with you about this all day," I said.

"Ah," said Toshi, "But I have a commitment that I must soon meet. So I will make you an invitation; come to my home at 7:00 p.m. this evening, if you wish, after you have your dinner. I will have a cigar for us and we will continue our talk then. I think you will appreciate it if you are able to come."

"I would like that very much," I said.

"Excellent," Toshi said. "I do not live far from here." He took a napkin from the table and wrote down his address and drew a simple map for directions. He stood up, bowed to me, picked up his book and walked away.

I arrived at Toshi's house, a small two-story bungalow on a verdant hillside less than a quarter mile from the beach, a little before seven. Toshi answered the door when I knocked. He invited me in and took me upstairs to a room over the one-car garage. We entered through a door at the rear of the room. There was a pair of open French doors at the opposite end of the room revealing a sweeping view of the ocean. There was a wooden table with four chairs in the center of the room, and a slow-rotating fan above it on the high ceiling. The room itself was plain, with wood paneling on one side. There was a painting of what appeared to be a Buddhist temple on one side wall. Two long silk prints with Japanese calligraphy hung above a sideboard against the opposite wall. At the rear wall was a small alter that included a sitting Buddha, incense and a bonsai tree. There were a couple of mats and some pillows and cushions used for meditation on the floor, but not much else. The décor was simplicity and the ambiance tranquility.

Toshi asked me if I had trouble finding his house. I said I did not. I then heard the sound of footsteps approaching from the back stairs. As I turned from the view of the ocean I saw Toshi bow to greet a man and a woman as they entered the room.

"Welcome," Toshi said. They both returned his bow. He then introduced me to James and Lea.

"James and Lea will join us this evening to enjoy a cigar and review our practice," said Toshi. "We do this from time to time, and tonight you will participate in our discussion."

At that Toshi brought out a wooden box and had us all place our watches and phones inside of it. He looked at me and said, "No distractions when we talk," and placed the box inside the sideboard. He then asked us to have a seat at the table.

Toshi went back into the sideboard and brought out four cigars, two ashtrays, a cutter and long wooden matches. He placed the cigars on the table and asked us to each select one; he took the remaining cigar. As he took his cigar he held it out in front of him and asked us to regard ours, and the effort that went into their making. When we had prepared our cigars for lighting, Toshi lit a match and passed it to James on his right. James toasted the foot, lit his cigar and passed the lit match to Lea on his right. Lea did the same and handed me the lit match. I followed suit and with the match nearing its end, passed it to Toshi.

With his cigar now lit, Toshi looked at me and said, "To begin our discussions, I ask if anyone has a thought or question concerning an aspect our Zen practice, or an experience that had an effect on them they wish to share and explore. As our guest, we offer you the opportunity to begin."

All eyes were on me as I drew on my cigar and exhaled; the draw was perfect, providing an abundance of creamy smoke with hints of chocolate and spice. "There is so much to understand about Zen," I said, "But it seems that at its center it is about 'acceptance'. I suppose my question is - acceptance of what, exactly, and to what degree?"

Toshi looked at Lea and James; then to me he said, "This is a very important matter. The answer is acceptance of life in total, including accepting oneself in total. There can be no partial acceptance for there to be oneness, and thus freedom."

"What is the difference?" I said.

"Attempting to accept life in total seems futile because we are constantly at odds with whatever seems to go against us. This is because in attempting to be one with life we are trying to gain that which we do not realize already exists. So our attempts to attain it become impediments by strengthening the belief that we are separated from life and have to unite with it. Over the millennia we have separated ourselves from nature, outside and inside of us, making us believe that we are independent and autonomous – that we are in control.

"Everything is constantly changing, but we refuse to accept a change if it is not to our liking; so we resist. But we are not in control! We therefore become frustrated and create our own suffering. When we accept the change, which is none other than life itself, we are living in the present moment. For the only thing we can control is our self.

"Having lost our connection with nature we must recognize our separation before we can accept life in total, which includes accepting ourselves."

"What does it mean to accept oneself?" Lea said.

Without accepting your full self - the existence of your inner demons along with your inner saints - together with the exterior world, your acceptance is only partial.

"If I accept life am I not accepting myself as well?" I said.

"The process is the same," Toshi said, "But acceptance of our exterior life involves acceptance of every situation we encounter and acceptance of our inner self involves intimate introspection.

"It is total acceptance of *all* of your feelings and thoughts, including the darkest most venal urges and desires of your subconscious when they surface. You will try to repress them, because you do not want them to be a part of you, but then they will only surface later even stronger. You do this because you believe you must be in control. When you cannot keep them from returning, this inner conflict creates your suffering. So you must acknowledge the fact that you have such dark feelings and thoughts and accept them. But accepting that you have them does mean that you must act on them. We know that it is a waste of our time, and that there is no value in doing so. So we acknowledge such thoughts when they come and let them pass like the clouds in the sky. With acceptance of yourself in whole, together with acceptance of your external world, you are free to be happy."

Toshi nodded, drew on his cigar, held a moment and blew out a large plume of smoke.

At this Lea said, "But how do we accept every situation?"

Toshi regarded his cigar and then said, "By pursuing the proper situational dictate. Accept without opposition, blame or attachment. Then take the necessary action spontaneously, without thinking, reacting only to the present situational dictate."

"What do you mean by 'situational dictate'" I said.

"Every moment we face a different situation, and each moment deserves our attention and each situation requires our action. But our action should be spontaneous, without regard for psychological time," said Toshi.

James, who had been quietly smoking and listening, said, "How do you mean, without regard for psychological time?"

"Let us say that you have taken your young child to the amusement park and she is on a ride that malfunctions. She is thrown to the ground and begins to cry in pain. You do not stop to admonish yourself for allowing her on the ride. You do not think about the safety of the ride. You do not think about how you will seek retribution or restitution from the amusement park owner, or of the hospital bills you may incur or of any school she may miss as a result of the accident. You only rush to her to assess her condition and immediately do what must be done to ease her pain and fix her problem. Anything added is a waste of time that can make the problem worse."

"So we don't think, we just act," I said.

"Yes!" said Toshi. "Acceptance does not mean to be passive. In such a situation you think only of the moment, taking appropriate action for the situation at hand with no regard for yourself. This is the right practice. You accept and do. Enlightenment, or wisdom, is found by complete acceptance of where you are at each moment. From there the journey continues. This is the realization of your true nature."

We all sat silent for a moment as we absorbed what Toshi had just said. As he had been doing most of the talking, Toshi now took the opportunity to sit back and enjoy his cigar. The rest of us did the same. I took a puff and as the smoke rose I felt as though I was right there with it. The moment became a few minutes of enjoying our cigars, which were past the halfway point when James posed a question to the group that began a discussion about non-duality. That discussion took us to the end of our cigars and the conclusion of our talks.

As Toshi declared our talks at an end, he placed his cigar butt in an ashtray and the three of us followed suit. He said that he appreciated our participation. I asked if we could help him clean up and he told me no, that he would do that after we had gone. He then brought the wooden box from the sideboard and we retrieved our belongings. Toshi bowed to each of us and we returned his bow. He told us he hoped to see each of us again soon. He then walked us downstairs and saw us to the door.

As I was about to leave Toshi said, "I hope you found your time with us enjoyable."

"I did, very much so," I said.

"Do not forget your zazen," he said, as he closed the door.

Unfortunately, I have not had the occasion to visit that little town again, and have not seen Toshi since that wonderful evening. But I will always remember him.

ZEN CIGAR SESSHIN STRUCTURE

Sesshin Basics

The basic requirements for conducting a Zen Cigar Sesshin (ZCS) are as follows:

- An appropriate location to hold a Sesshin.

- A maximum of four people. A Sesshin may include fewer than four but there should not more than four.

- A Host. One of the four attendees will be referred to as the Host prior to and during the Sesshin.

- Participant. The other attendees will be referred to as Participants before and during the Sesshin.

- Eight premium, hand-rolled cigars and appropriate smoking paraphernalia. The suggested cigar size is a Toro, with a Robusto being the minimum size.

- A pitcher of water and/or cold tea.

Pre Sesshin

It is expected that someone who attends a ZCS practices Zen and smokes cigars. One knows whether they practice Zen, but may question if they are a cigar smoker depending on how much or how little they smoke. The fact is, someone who smokes just two or three cigars per month is a cigar smoker, as long as they enjoy their cigars. On the other hand, if someone smokes cigars only to "fit in" or to "get ahead," this is not the right practice and they will not be in harmony with the intention of the ZCS. Regardless of how many cigars a person smokes, they should enjoy and appreciate the cigars they do smoke. If not they should not smoke them.

If a person practices Zen but does not smoke cigars, they should not take up cigar smoking merely to attend the ZCS. However, a practitioner of Zen could smoke a cigar outside of the ZCS to see if they enjoy and appreciate the experience. If they find it enjoyable and relaxing they may then wish to pursue it and attend a ZCS sometime in the future. This is their investigation and the right practice. By the same token, a cigar smoker who knows nothing of Zen must first become familiar with the principals of Zen Buddhism before attending a ZCS. Thus, at minimum a rudimentary knowledge of Zen and of smoking cigars is necessary for participating in a ZCS. Only with this knowledge and experience will a person be in harmony with the intention of the ZCS.

Preparation

It is recommended that Participants have a meal prior to and in preparation for a ZCS. The consumption of food will provide stamina for the Participants to function best during the discussions, and preclude any distraction resulting from a feeling of hunger during the duration of their attendance. It will also mitigate any potential lightheadedness that can occur while smoking a cigar on an empty stomach. In general, a meal before the proceedings will help foster a feeling of contentment and relaxation to help ensure a meaningful and productive discussion.

Prior to the ZCS Participants may decide if they wish to take their meal together or individually. The Host will contact and poll the Participants in advance to determine whether they wish to dine together or separately; if together, a place and time will be agreed upon and each person will be responsible for the cost of their own meal. If it is agreed that the Participants will eat separately they will do so and then arrive at the location of the ZCS at the appropriate time.

Should the Participants decide to dine together, it is suggested that any conversation not involve the topic of Zen or issues similar to those to be discussed at the ZCS. Such matters are best reserved for the ZCS itself. Similarly, if two or more of the Participants do dine together prior to the ZCS, the location of their meal should not be the same as the location of the ZCS itself. There should be no thought or concern of anything having to do with the meal taken immediately before, such as cleaning up or the need to return to the site of the meal for any reason once the Participants enter the place of the ZCS. Thus, an off-site location for the meal would be best.

For example, the meal should not take place at the residence of a Host if the ZCS which follows will take place at the same residence. A nearby restaurant would be preferable. If the ZCS is to be held at a hotel, it would be acceptable for all to dine together at the hotel as long as the ZCS is held in a hotel room or patio area well out of sight and earshot from the location of the meal. Again, this is intended to avoid thoughts or attachment to anything having had to do with the meal; such as quality, quantity, clean up, service, etc.

Whether Participants eat together or separately it is recommended that no alcohol is consumed during the meal. This will ensure clear heads and a productive discussion for all in attendance at the ZCS to follow.

The Meeting Space

The location of the room or area where the ZCS takes place should be somewhere the Participants will not be disturbed for any reason during the time they meet. Nor should their presence disturb anyone else. The location should be quiet, without distractions or noises emanating from either inside or outside the space. The space should have good ventilation of one form or another to avoid it becoming too smoky or stuffy. The smoke, once ventilated from the space, should not annoy non-smokers in the vicinity; interruptions resulting from external complaints during the discussions would be counterproductive. Weather permitting, outdoor venues such as back yards or lanais could work well, depending on other ambient conditions.

Entering the ZCS

Regardless of the location of the ZCS, Participants should enter its confines one at a time through a specified point of ingress/egress.

Just prior to or immediately upon entering, each Participant must disconnect from the modern-day world. This is done by placing all items and devices that connect them to it in a single receptacle, provided and secured by the Host, preferably just outside the point of entry. Such items include but are not limited to: car keys, house keys, watches, pagers, cell phones, smart phones, electronic tablets, e-books, Mp3 music players, etc. Participants shall retrieve all items at the conclusion of their discussions.

Wearing articles of clothing with logos or insignias is to be avoided, as are hats, tank tops, short skirts and dresses. Participants should also refrain from wearing/using perfume or cologne and noisy jewelry. Hosts should not burn incense or play music during the Sesshin either. The intent is to establish an environment of tranquility, with no distractions whatsoever, where all individuals are equal, without station, privilege or allegiance. Only in this fashion can the ZCS be truly meaningful.

Although there is to be no food of any kind consumed during a ZCS, the Host should provide something for Participants to drink for hydration, or just to "wet the whistle," as talking can tend to dry ones mouth. To that end, the Host should provide water and/or cold tea. The beverages should not be placed on the table where the discussions occur. They should instead be located in proximity to the table in nondescript service containers or pitchers.

Once Inside

If the Host is not already inside the meeting area when the Participants arrive, or if the Host arrives with the Participants, the Host should go inside before the others so as to greet them when they enter. Inside the confines of the ZCS area the Host takes on particular responsibilities in leading the Participants during the ZCS. As Participants enter they will be greeted by the Host. The Host will bow one time to the Participant and the Participant will return the bow. That Participant will then bow to each of the other Participants already there and they will return the bow.

Bowing has important significance; by bowing we are giving up ourselves. To give up ourselves means to give up our dualistic ideas – our ego. This is the right attitude for a ZCS. It is a show of humility, a demonstration which indicates that we are no better than the one to whom we bow. Here we bow to acknowledge our oneness with all things and to signify that our mind is open and ready to listen completely and without discrimination. Without this strong conviction our bow is dualistic. Bowing helps rid ourselves of our self-centered ideas, which is not easy to do. Bowing is a reminder. We may not be used to it, feeling it is more appropriate for Eastern cultures. But in our daily life we should also continue to bow, if only in our minds. It brings calmness to our Being. This is why we first bow at the ZCS. This is a worthwhile practice and the ZCS is a time to remember this.

Inside the meeting space there will be a table with the number of chairs around it that correspond to the number of Participants. On the table the Host will have placed a number of premium hand rolled cigars - two cigars per Participant. The cigars will be arrayed in a circle with an equidistant space between each cigar. It is the Host's duty to obtain and lay out the cigars prior to the Participants' arrival. The Host will also have removed the bands from the cigars prior to placing them on the table.

The reason for removing the bands is to preclude the Participants from having any ideas about the cigars to be smoked. By removing the bands we remove any dualistic thoughts about the cigars; good or bad, quality or not, etc. They are all to be premium handmade cigars and thus quality cigars. All of the cigars will be exactly the same: brand, style, size, shape and strength – mild, medium or full bodied.

Because cigar smokers have different preferences regarding the strength of cigars they like to smoke, a suggestion would be to choose the middle path and provide medium bodied cigars for a ZCS. Doing so should not disappoint someone who prefers full bodied cigars, as there is ample flavor in a premium medium bodied smoke. And a medium bodied cigar, although slightly stronger than a mild bodied one, should not overpower someone who smokes mild cigars. A person who smokes medium bodied cigars should be quite content.

For their future smoking knowledge, the Host will provide the Participants with the cigar bands at the conclusion of the ZCS.

With all present and the cigars properly arrayed, the Host will ask the Participants to select their cigars. They may view all cigars and then select any two they wish. This selection process takes place with all Participants simultaneously. Once all Participants have made their selections and removed their cigars from the table, the Host will take the remaining two cigars. If the smoking paraphernalia is not already on the table the Host will retrieve it and place it there now. This includes: appropriately sized ash trays, wooden matches, butane lighters and cedar spills if possible. (Cedar spills may be purchased in tobacco stores, or may be made from the thin cedar dividers that come in many cigar boxes). The quantity, or number, of items to be provided should be adequate to facilitate an easy and relaxed smoking experience.

The length of the ZCS is determined by the duration of the simultaneous smoking by the Participants of one cigar each. Should a cigar, at any point, fail to provide a proper smoke to the satisfaction of a Participant, that person may set the faulty cigar aside and light his second cigar. Reasons for this would be if a cigar is plugged, booked, continue to go out, burn too hot, tastes bad, etc. Once done, the Participant will continue discourse along with the rest of the group. Of course, the rest of the group will likely finish their cigars first, expectedly close together, bringing a close to all smoking.

The second cigar, therefore, is back-up to ensure that all are able to continue to participate in the ZCS as intended, cigar in hand and stress free. At the end of the ZCS each Participant will keep their second cigar and take it with them. The intention is that when they smoke it later it will remind them to be calm, hopefully recall their previous Sesshin and thus reinforce their Zen practice.

When the Host has retrieved his cigars he will take his seat at the table first, before the other Participants sit. There is no specified seating arrangement for the Participants beyond the Host taking his seat prior to anyone else. Once all are seated the Host will bow to the Participants with a deep nod of the head and say aloud, "We begin." All Participants will return the bow, after which a Sesshin discussion point will be chosen.

It is the Host's responsibility to start the initial discussion. This may be done in one of two ways. The first way would be for the Host to select a point from one of the Sesshin Starters listed in this book, or to choose a relevant point of their own. The second way would be for the Host to defer to the Participants to have them agree among themselves on a topic, either from the Starters in the book or something from their own experience that is considered appropriate for discussion. When a discussion point has been chosen the Host will move on to the lighting of cigars.

At this time all Participants, including the Host, will take a moment to "appreciate" the cigar they are about to light, which after all is handmade and deserving of such appreciation for the time, process and craftsmanship that formed these small works of art. No more than a moment is needed to view the wrapper, feel the firmness and savor the aroma.

The process for lighting cigars at the ZCS is in accordance with the proper etiquette followed by aficionados everywhere. To begin, each Participant will clip their cigars with the clippers supplied by the Host and place the clippings in one of the ash trays. Each will then char the foot of their own cigar with their choice of a wooden match or butane lighter, also supplied by the Host. Once this is done the Host will light a cedar spill and use it to light his own cigar. He will then pass the lit spill to the Participant on his right who will use it to light his cigar then pass it to his right, and so on. If necessary, before the original spill can go out, a second one should be lit from the first one, and the second one should then be used to light any remaining cigars. The significance of using one flame to light all cigars is two-fold; it embodies the best cigar smoking etiquette and practice, and it symbolizes the unity of all those present. (As spills may not always be available, a long wooden match will suffice). During the proceedings should an individual need to relight their cigar for whatever reason, or need to light their second cigar, they may do so with a match or lighter, whichever they prefer.

While smoking during the ZCS Participants should take their time and smoke slowly and peacefully in accordance with the ambience of the Sesshin. They should avoid smoking like the proverbial chimney. It is usually best when all Participants finish their cigars approximately together, signaling the close of the discussions.

During smoking Participants should refrain from commenting on their cigars, as the time is limited and the conversation is to explore and further their Zen practice.

To simply appreciate the cigars and their calming affects without attaching to them is the right practice.

Along the same line, one of the qualities of a good cigar is the length of ash it may produce. Given the opportunity, a smoker of a premium handmade cigar can generate a very long ash. But doing so does not necessarily enhance the smoking. During the ZCS, doing so would be considered attaching to a gaining or grasping idea. It would not be humble; there is no competition. So in the ZCS we do not let an ash become more than an inch in length. This is an example of something the Host may point out should it occur.

Concluding the Sesshin

The ZCS will end when the Host indicates that the cigars have been sufficiently exhausted and the discussion has run its course. At that point he will ask the Participants to put down their cigars. He will stand and bow to those at the table and thank them for participating.

They will return his bow and then get up from the table. The Host will then provide each Participant with a cigar band from the cigars they just smoked. They will then file out and retrieve the items they left outside the room. It is the Host's responsibility to clean and restore the meeting space after the participants have left.

SESSHIN DISCUSSSION
&
STARTERS

After years of searching, the Buddha identified the cause of man's suffering and provided the way to end it. He realized man's alienation from life – man's inability to recognize his true nature, his oneness with the universe. The Buddha conveyed this truth to his first disciple through "direct pointing" by merely holding up a flower without speaking, because he knew that words could not transmit his personal revelation. Everyone must discover their true nature for themselves.

Subsequently he did memorialize his Four Noble Truths and his Eightfold Path that when followed, before or after awakening, increases the wisdom that functions as compassion; the wisdom of oneness that brings spiritual freedom and happiness through the acceptance of life as it presents itself. When followed, these *dharma*, together with Buddha's Pure Precepts, helps us keep the ego in check. This, in the broadest sense, is the principal intention of the ZCS – discussions concerning how our ego affects us, how we can become aware of its effort to control us and how we can contain it and put an end to our *dukkha*.

The following pages contain Sesshin Starters to facilitate beginning a conversation at the commencement of a ZCS, or at any time necessary during a Sesshin.

Sesshin Starters

A Sesshin Starter should be viewed from any perspective; as though it is a question, a statement, a comment, an implication or just an invitation to spark a thought, which when expressed will prompt the flow of discourse around the table in an enlightening discussion.

Sesshin Starters are just that, starters. Once a Starter has been addressed the topic should continue to be explored; why is such and such acceptable, what would unacceptable be? How are we affected, how does such action affect us individually and collectively? How do we avoid the inappropriate and ensure the appropriate? Or, cite personal examples and explore the examples given.

- When there is no gaining idea in what you do, then you are doing something. When there is a gaining idea in what you do, then you are doing nothing.

- The ego keeps us from -

- We are not our ego because –

- We stop the ego by -

- We disengage the ego by -

- When we expose the ego -

- The ego can't solve our problems because -

- Compassion is -

- To 'leave no trace' is to -

- We 'leave no trace' by -

- We maintain a beginner's mind by -

- We attach to -

- We attach because -

- Our ego sees us in opposition to –

- Attachment affects our thinking by –

- We stop attaching by –

- Attachment affects our actions by -

- When we attach to our past we portray ourselves as -

- Our perception affects our activity by -

- We fail to let things go as they go because –

- When we fail to let things go as they go -

- When our desire controls our feelings -

- We keep our desire from controlling our feelings -

- Not knowing is -

- The importance of not knowing is -

- Through not knowing we achieve –

- Through not knowing we function as

- Our attachment to the ego renders us spiritually -

- The past and future only exist -

- By not reacting to another's ego we -

- Discriminating is the wrong practice when -

- Labeling things creates expectations causing dukkha by -

- Dualistic thinking causes dukkha by -

- When you are hot go where the heat is. When you are cold go where the cold is, is to -

- Live in the Absolute and Relative worlds simultaneously by-

- Everything is the same yet everything is different because -

- Our ideas, concepts and notions restrict us by -

- Who is in control?

- To realize our true nature we -

- We are motivated to seek our oneness by -

- We are ignorant when we –

- To resist the present moment is to -

- Accepting all pairs of opposites every moment we -

- Preoccupation with the past and future preclude us from -

- The first step in diminishing the ego is to -

- Eliminate self-craving by -

- Eliminating self-craving we -

- At its core the ego creates and perpetuates our -

- Acceptance of the three signs of Being we -

- Enlightenment and Awakening are merely words, notions and as such are dualistic. We avoid this dualism by -

- We realize the world as emptiness by –

- To attach to the past is to invite -

- We are we who we truly are when -

- Manifest who we truly are by -

- Psychological time affects us by -

- To address any situation properly we must-

- Can anything actually change who we truly are?

- Wood that burns does not become ashes because -

- Acceptance is freedom by -

- Satisfaction can only be defined by suffering is -

- Cope with fear of the future by -

- The ego controls when we identify with -

- "Just as it is" describes -

- The state of no separation is –

- Living in the present we don't do these three things -

- The function of wisdom is -

- The illusion is –

- The "suchness" of a thing is –

- To be unconscious is to identify with –

- When you are conscious you are –

- To remain conscious remain –

- Time is only a tool for operating in the -

- Past and future don't exist and create problems for us by –

- To attach to the past is to invite –

- Acceptance is living in the –

- When we are mindful there are no deleterious effects from –

- Fear is create by our attachment to –

- If we are not happy we are not living in –

- We question our thoughts, reactions and emotions to remain-

- To observe the ego is to –

- Consciousness is abandonment of our

- Dissolving the ego we manifest our -

For Sesshin Starter responses email:
pppatdp@gmail.com

ESTABLISH YOUR OWN ZEN CIGAR SESSHIN

Now that you understand the academics of the ZCS, short for Zen Cigar Sesshin, it is time to begin participating in our own discussion groups. But where do you find one? It may be difficult at first to locate an established ZCS group, which means you will need to be proactive initially and most likely establish one.

Initially it would make sense to contact like-minded family members, friends and acquaintances and to suggest that they do the same. Should you be in reasonable proximity to an existing Zen Center, call or visit the Center and explain your intention, focusing on speaking with their cigar smoking members. Mention the book as a way of introducing the topic. Next you may consider visiting the cigar stores in your area and speaking with the proprietor and store's regular patrons regarding the ZCS. There may even be a possibility of conducting a ZCS at one such store. Many have individual smoking rooms or areas that may accommodate discussion group.

Finally, there is always social media for a more expansive query for those comfortable and proficient with use of that medium.

Remember, just be and do – nothing special.

PROLOGUE
TO
PRIMERS

For me, two of the most satisfying things are Zen and a good cigar. Both are natural and on the surface each appears fairly straightforward; Zen is simply living and doing in the present moment – here and now, and a cigar is merely rolled tobacco. Yet each is complex in its own way. As with many things in life the details lie below the surface and only through patient investigation are those details revealed. For example, to the naked eye any particular cigar may appear fine, but upon being lit it may refuse to draw as a result of being rolled too tightly. Or it may draw too easily, the tobacco having not been rolled tight enough, and thus burn too hot for the tongue. Or it may continue to go out and taste bad during smoking due to latent veins or stems. With a quick visual and tactile inspection by a seasoned cigar aficionado these issues and others may be avoided and a smokable cigar readily selected. But when something is unavoidably missed and your last cigar turns out to be a dud, frustrating what was anticipated to be a relaxing smoke, this is when living a Zen lifestyle is helpful.

One of Zen's principal truths is that you cannot control anything in life other than yourself. Accepting this, your frustration level is immediately and substantially reduced. Zen also says that since you can't control a situation you should not resist it. So you would not tear up the faulty stogie to determine the cause of its failure, you would not be able to enjoy it even if you did. Zen also says not to judge or attach to a situation. So you don't blame the merchant that sold it to you, or the roller who constructed it, or even the company for which he or she works. And once you have finally tossed the cigar in question you don't think of it again because it is now in the past, and for the Zen mind there is no past. The only thing that exists is the present moment, and you can't live in the present if you dwell in the past.

It takes time to learn about and understand cigars: the tobaccos involved for each part of the cigar, what part of the plant they come from, their geographic origin and how these things combine to affect flavor; ring gauge, length and shape or style and how each affects the smoking process; the particular aging process used in curing; machine or handmade, etc. Like anything else, the only way to learn is through experience.

The same is true of Zen. The example above involving how to deal with an impaired cigar, although seemingly as simple as presented, can be difficult in practice, particularly for Westerners due to our brand of societal convention, that is, our way of thinking. Really, who could just toss their last premium cigar without a second thought the moment they were about to enjoy it? A practitioner of Zen could and would find it liberating. The Zen principals employed in the example above work the same for any situation. Of course, being a way of life one needs to understand Zen, which can take a lifetime. At some point living Zen we may experience Enlightenment – the realization of our oneness with all things - which may occur after many long years of specific types of practice or suddenly and spontaneously. Or it may not occur at all. But Enlightenment is not Zen's goal because Zen has no goals. Zen is simply living moment by moment day by day, as thoughtfully and mindfully as possible. Doing this makes one a better person, enlightened or not, who in turn will affect others in a positive way and ultimately help make the world a better place. For Zen this is the destiny for all sentient beings.

This is not to diminish the noble cigar, something Zen would never do, which again, is complex in its own right. The cigar also needs understanding to be appreciated so that rather than just having a smoke, one may enjoy the experience of a "Smoke." To some this comes naturally over time, to others not so much. This is not to say that one may not take their cigar as they see fit, but there is a difference between smoking and a Smoke. One smokes a cigar as an affectation or when he or she is not completely relaxed and where the ambiance around the smoker takes precedence over the experience of smoking; such as during a game of golf out on the links, in a crowded and noisy bar where one must virtually shout just to be heard, or riding in a convertible with the top down, etc. Anyone may smoke a cigar in these scenarios but the savvy smoker wouldn't necessarily be smoking top shelf sticks.   It would be a waste because the subtleties of a premium cigar would be lost under such circumstances. Typically premium cigars are reserved for a "Smoke". How does a Smoke differ from a smoke? Used herein a Smoke begins with the intention of separating oneself from the chaos of the rest of the world for the duration of a single specific cigar. At the same time the smoker embraces a feeling of tranquility for himself and respect for the attributes of the cigar he is about to enjoy.   Thereafter, whether alone or with colleagues, and without haste, he follows the proper protocol and etiquette for preparing, lighting, smoking and mindfully enjoying the cigar.   Unlike a smoke, where the ambiance around the smoker takes precedence over the experience of smoking, during a Smoke the ambiance is integral to the experience of smoking and a concordance occurs with smoker, cigar and surroundings creating oneness among all three.   At the conclusion of a Smoke the smoker's tranquility remains for some time thereafter.

It would seem natural then that Zen practitioners who are also cigar Smokers would recognize the Zen Cigar Sesshin's potential benefits in furtherance of one's Zen practice.

It is believed important, however, to include a brief primer on both Zen and cigars in this book. While it is not anticipated that a participant of a Zen Cigar Sesshin would know nothing of Zen or cigars, someone who knows less of one or the other should benefit by a review of either or both of the following primers prior to attending. But as indicated, these are brief, particularly for Zen, and the reader is urged to seek other more complete and thorough subject writings elsewhere.

ZEN PRIMER

INSIDE ZEN

What is Zen   59

Zen History   61

Enlightenment 85

Meditation   89

Living Zen   104

Metta Buddha 111

WHAT IS ZEN

"It is not good to talk about Zen because Zen is nothingness . . . If you talk about it you are always lying, and if you don't talk about it no one knows it is there."
- Robert Pirsig

What is Zen? That is the question. The word is ubiquitous today, found everywhere and in everything, from cook books to T.V. shows and movies, from restaurant take-out menus to design software for websites. Some think they know, some want to know and those that do know don't say anything.

But what *is* Zen, really? It's simple - just be and do - that is Zen. It is living in the present moment and being mindful, but with no mind, and calming nervous energy through *zazen* with no objective other than to sit and breathe.

Of course, the full depth and breadth of the more than twenty-five hundred year history of Zen Buddhism could never be summed up so simply. Or could it?

It is expected that from time to time people with little or no exposure to Zen may be invited to attend a Zen Cigar Sesshin by experienced Zen practitioners. It is important for someone participating to have at least a general understanding of Zen for their experience to be meaningful. A read of this primer, which can barely be considered a wink and a nod in the direction of Zen, should be enough for a novice to participate in a Zen Cigar Sesshin with some level of comfort. Thereafter, with further investigation and practice, including Zen Cigar Sesshin discussions, that person should be able to appreciate and effectively contribute to future Zen Cigar Sesshin discussions.

ZEN HISTORY

"Someone who seeks the Way doesn't look beyond himself." – Bodhidharma

Zen is a sect of Buddhism that arrived in Japan from China in the seventh-century as an outgrowth of a combination of Indian Mahayana Buddhism and Chinese Taoism. The word Zen is Japanese for "meditation," (*Dhyana* in Sanskrit and *Ch'an* in Chinese). It originated with Indian Buddhism. Buddhism originated in India with a man named Siddhartha Gautama approximately five-hundred years before the birth of Jesus Christ.

Gautama was born a prince into a wealthy ruling class family. His father, wishing to ensure that his son grew up to be a king rather than a holy man, prevented him from ever leaving the palace, where Gautama never encountered suffering of any sort. But when he was 29 his curiosity got the best of him. Despite his father's efforts, and without his knowledge, Gautama left and returned to the palace on four separate occasions. On each occasion he encountered ordinary people suffering; the first time an old man, the second time a sick man, the third time a corpse and the fourth time an ascetic beggar, seemingly at peace and content with the world. After seeing these things Gautama abandoned his life of privilege and began a quest for spiritualism and a way to end suffering.

Initially Gautama studied religions with and learned meditation from the well-known religious sages of the time and mastered it all. In doing so he did not find the truth he sought or the way to permanently end suffering; so he continued his quest.

Next he practiced intense asceticism, almost starving himself in the process before realizing that it was not the way to end suffering. Then, one day as he was given something to eat by a village boy, he made the decision to focus his effort on the use of a specific meditative style to find his answers. In doing so Gautama discovered the Middle Way, the way of living by moderation, between the extremes of excess and self-denial.

At the age of 35, and after six years of searching, Gautama one day proclaimed that he would not rise from his meditation under the Bodhi tree until he had learned how to eradicate all suffering in the world. After meditating the entire night he arose at the break of dawn – he had attained nirvana. This was the "unexcelled, complete awakening." Upon his enlightenment the Buddha declared: "How wonderful! Everything as it is is enlightened!" He was now fully enlightened and had realized the universal law of cause and effect, or *karma*, and the oneness of the universe as well as the cause of all suffering and how to end it.

Upon his enlightenment the Buddha was filled with a profound empathy for all sentient beings. He went on to teach the truths he had realized, referred to as *dharma* by Buddhists, until his death at about the age of 80. Soon after his enlightenment the Buddha brought his close followers together and set forth his *dharma* by way of the Four Noble Truths and the means of implementing them through his Noble Eightfold Path.

The Four Noble Truths

At the center of the Buddha's *dharma* are the Four Noble Truths. They identify suffering as the main problem confronting humans, explain why they encounter it and how it may be eliminated. Here they are in brief:

· The First Noble Truth

It says life is *dukkha*, or suffering. *Dukkha* is Sanskrit for suffering regardless of the source. It is the sense or feeling that something is just not right. We feel our life is lacking something, wonder why we aren't happy with what we have, or that others are better off than us. At other times it is very clear, as when we are injured physically or emotionally. All of this is *dukkha* or suffering.

· **The Second Noble Truth**

It explains the cause for our suffering. It says that suffering is caused by our grasping and our desire. It is desire for something we want, don't have or wish was different. It's a clinging to something we find desirable and an aversion to something we find undesirable. A grasping idea that if we only had this or that that our life would somehow be better. It is a general discontent with the current state of affairs.

· **The Third Noble Truth**

It says that we can eliminate suffering by eliminating our grasping ideas, our desire.

· **The Fourth Noble Truth**

It tells us to follow the Eightfold Path in order to rid ourselves of desire. Following the Eightfold Path mitigates our desires and grasping ideas and thus eases our suffering;

less suffering more happiness. We follow the Eightfold Path before and after our enlightenment.

It is important to know that the Sanskrit word *dukkha*, as used by the Buddha, was not limited to our meaning of suffering. The Buddha taught that there are three types of *dukkha*: Suffering, impermanence and conditioned states.

1. Normal suffering is *dukkha*, and includes physical, mental and emotional pain.

2. If something is not permanent then it is subject to change, and is *dukkha*. Our physical beauty is *dukkha* because it will age and change with time. Our most joyful times are *dukkha* because they will not last. It is fine to delight in the joyful times, just don't cling to them.

3. To be affected by or dependent on something else is to be conditioned. The Buddha taught that all phenomena are conditioned. Everything affecting everything else creates *dukkha*.

To better appreciate the Four Noble Truths and the Noble Eightfold Path it is necessary to understand two of the Buddha's basic teachings, which are: "no self" and the "*Skandhas*" – the "five aggregates" sometimes called the "five conditions".   In brief, Buddha taught the doctrine of *anatman* – that there is no self in the sense of a permanent, integral, autonomous being within an individual existence; and of the *skandhas*, or five aggregates, a combination of five properties or energies that comprise what we consider an individual being. The Five *Skandhas* are:

1. **Form**, *Rupa* – is matter or material we can sense. These include our physical bodies in their entirety.

2. **Sensation**, *Vedana* – a physical or mental sensation we have through contact with our senses: Body with material things, eye with visible form, ear with sound, nose with odor, tongue with taste, mind with thoughts or notions.

3. **Perception**, *Samjna* – is the faculty

that recognizes. Our thinking ability for conceptualization and association.

4. **Mental Formation**, *Samskara* – Volition

5. **Consciousness**, *Vijnana* – this is a re-action with one of the faculties as the basis and its corresponding phenomena as the object, i.e. eye and sight, mind and thought, etc.

What we think of as our self, our ego and our personality, are temporary creations of the *skandhas* and are not permanent.

The Noble Eightfold Path

Following the Noble Eightfold Path is the way to obtain the knowledge through which one may encounter self-awakening and realize the unity of all things. Buddhism groups the eight principals in three divisions: Wisdom includes 1 and 2; Ethical Conduct includes 3, 4 and 5; and Concentration includes 6, 7 and 8. To follow the Noble Eightfold Path is to eliminate suffering from our lives.

The eight principals are as follows:

· **Right Understanding**

Right understanding provides direction and usefulness for the other seven principals. It stipulates that life is not permanent, that our suffering is a result of our grasping and that our grasping or desire is tied to the wrong belief that we lack something. Right understanding may also be viewed as knowing the oneness, or unity, of all sentient beings and the truth of *karma.*

· **Right Thought**

Right thought means thinking without malice. It means aiming to rid oneself of thoughts that are inherently wrong or depraved or generally unkind.

· **Right Speech**

Right speech is to refrain from lying, from contentious or offensive speech, or from talking just for attention or to agitate someone. One's speech should be thoughtful, kind and kept to a minimum.

· Right Action

Right action means right conduct and involves one's sense of morality. It means to not kill, steal in any fashion, engage in sexual misconduct or to abuse the use of intoxicants.

· Right Livelihood

Right livelihood means that one should not engage in trades or occupations which either directly or indirectly result in the harm of other living beings. Our livelihood should be ethical and honest and should not be made by cheating or stealing. It should be considerate of all living things and foster love and compassion for all sentient beings. The five professions Buddhists consider not being right livelihood are trading in weapons, people (prostitution or slavery), meat (killing and butchering of animals), alcohol or drugs and poison.

Right livelihood also means

that we do not judge other based on
what they do.

· Right Effort

Right effort is to try to prevent
our unhealthy or negative thoughts
and qualities and to dismiss them
whenever they do arise. It is also to
make a concerted effort to establish
and maintain healthy and positive
qualities in oneself.

· Right Mindfulness

Right mindfulness means
continually working to remain in
the present open, quiet, and alert. It
means continual awareness of what
our body is doing, our surroundings
and of our feelings. As thoughts
come just acknowledge them and
then let them go. It is akin to our
eyes being able to focus while
the peripheral vision maintains a
constant vigilance of the vicinity.

· Right Concentration

Right concentration is to
develop the ability to focus totally

on whatever we do as we are doing it. The ability to do this is achieved by the discipline gained through the continued practice of meditation. This total focus of the task at hand will help eliminate grasping, desire, and other distractions that keep us from living in the present, which will make our life more rewarding.

The Three Treasures

The three treasures tie everything up for Buddhists. They are the three things where they can retreat and find support. The treasures are:

- The Buddha.
- The *dharma* – Buddha's teachings.
- The sangha – the followers of Buddhism.

Buddhism + Tao = Zen

Bodhidharma (470-543 A.D.) was born in India and was the twenty-eighth Patriarch in a lineage traced directly back to Gautama Buddha himself. He became a follower of Mahayana Buddhism under the twenty-seventh Patriarch, Prajnatara, and traveled to China early in the sixth century. By this time Buddhism had already been in China for a couple of hundred years.

Bodhidharma is normally depicted as a large man with a perpetual scowl and a long aquiline nose. He became known as the blue-eyed demon in China because he looked so different with his Aryan appearance and large blue eyes.

Bodhidharma's teachings in China are considered significant because of his departure from dependence on the *sutras* (Indian Buddhist scriptures), his style of directly pointing at the mind and his emphasis on sitting meditation to see into one's true nature to attain enlightenment. Specifically, Bodhidharma's individual brand of conveying the *dharma* was:

A special transmission outside the scriptures;

Not dependent on the written word;

Directly pointing to the mind;

Seeing into one's true nature and attaining Enlightenment.

Not long after arriving in China Bodhidharma meet with Emperor Wu of Liang, who although not impressed with Bodhidharma thought highly of the Buddhist concept. After the Emperor had funded the building of numerous Buddhist temples and contributed generously to the *Sangha* (the community of Buddhists at large) he asked Bodhidharma how much spiritual merit he had gained from all of the temples he had built and contributions he had made.

"None whatever," said Bodhidharma.

Then the Emperor asked Bodhidharma "What is the meaning of the dharma?"

"Empty," said Bodhidharma.

The Emperor finally asked Bodhidharma "Who are you?"

"I don't know," said Bodhidharma.

Upset at this point, the Emperor ousted Bodhidharma from the court.

Bodhidharma's curt, enigmatic responses to the Emperor's questions in this exchange are a foreshadowing of Zen's use of *koans* as a method of understanding the Buddha spirit. (*Koans* are seemingly illogical questions asked by Zen teachers of their students as a means for preparing them for enlightenment. It may take weeks or even years before a proper answer is given and the student may move on to another *koan*.)

After being sent from the court, Bodhidharma traveled to the Shaolin temple in what today is Henan Province of north China where the monks there refused him entry. It is said that he sat facing the temple walls, or in a nearby cave, meditating for nine years. He impressed the monks so much with his "sitting meditation" (*Tsu-chuan* in Chinese, *zazen* in Japanese) that they finally relented and allowed him into their temple.

Credited with the development of *Ch'an* (the Chinese word for Zen) in China, Bodhidharma is considered the

First Patriarch of Buddhism in China. Ultimately he chose a successor to transmit the *dharma* who chose a successor, and so forth. In all there were six patriarchs until the lineage ended.

The Sixth Patriarch was Hui-neng (638-713 A.D.), who many consider to be the real father of Zen due to his strong influence on it. His oversight, at the beginning of the T'ang Dynasty, signifies the beginning of what is still referred to as the "golden age" of Zen. Hui-neng was an uneducated woodcutter who showed a great inclination toward enlightenment. But when selected by the Fifth Patriarch to be the Sixth Patriarch the other better educated monks became quite upset. His life in danger, Hui-neng then fled without selecting his successor.

By this time Zen had found its own unique spirit, losing the arcane trappings of Indian Buddhism as it absorbed the *Tao*, which had a significant influence for living a more regular life. *Tao*, or "the Way," was a means of personal liberation in China.

The fundamental text of Taoism is the *Tao Te Ching,* written in the sixth century B.C., by Lao-Tzo. Taoism is the Chinese philosophy which seeks to liberate one from societal convention by following the *Tao* and through naturalness, spontaneity and simplicity in daily life. It was typically practiced by those at the end of their "conventional" or working life and during their "retirement". Following the Tao was a time for reflection and for insight into one's inner Being and oneness with the universe.

Ultimately, Ch'an spread to Vietnam, where it is called Thien, to Korea, where it is called Son and to Japan where it is called Zen.

Over time, Buddhism in China splintered into five different sects or schools. Two of those schools, known as Ts'ao Tung (Soto in Japanese) and Lin-chi (Rinzai in Japanese), were brought to Japan in the twelfth-century by Zen masters Dogen and Eisai, respectively. Both schools still have wide followings today in Japan and in the West.

The Soto school relies primarily on zazen to achieve enlightenment, where the Rinzai school relies most heavily on the practice of *koans*. That is not to say that *koans* are not used in the Soto school and that zazen is not practiced of in the Rinzai school, they are, but to lesser degrees.

So by the twelfth-century Zen had become embedded in the Japanese culture. As time passed Zen absorbed many aspects of Japanese tradition and was further refined. The Japanese emphasis on spontaneity and "no-mind" contributed heavily to Japan's approach to the arts.

Interestingly, Buddhism is barely practiced in India these days. Fortunately, Buddhism thrives in South East Asia today and has had a growing and important influence on Westerners ever since the end of World War II. Thus, long after its inception, with modifications to the good, Zen continues.

Zen in America

Japanese teachers introduced Zen in the United States at the end of the 19th century to serve groups of Japanese immigrants and to become acquainted with American culture. Subsequent to World War II, interest from non-Asian Americans quickly grew and started what would become an indigenous American Zen tradition. Since then there have been a good number of Zen experts, proponents, teachers and students. Here is a small group of some of the most influential and best known.

D. T. Suzuki

The first formal introduction of Zen into America was by Soyen Shaku in 1893 at the World Parliament of Religions in Chicago Illinois. But it was not until the late 1940s that Zen took hold with Daisetz T. Suzuki's (1870-1966) arrival in America and the publication of his writings. His message was focused on the meaning of enlightenment and the road leading to it. Because he lived in America with an American wife, his point of view enabled him to merge his native and adopted cultures allowing him to maintain a Zen life in a place among those with a minimal knowledge of Zen. He saw a great benefit in exposing the West to Eastern thought and vice versa. The bulk of his work was geared toward making Zen available to everybody, regardless of whom they were or where they lived.

Shunryu Suzuki

Shunryu Suzuki's (1905-1971) arrival in the U.S. in 1959 had a significant impact on Zen in this country. Suzuki practiced Soto Zen and his book, *Zen Mind, Beginners Mind*, provides insight into the practice of Zen for Americans and Western life alike. His book elaborates on the points of the Noble Eightfold Path and he stressed living with a "beginners mind" – like a child – as though everything is new and experienced for the first time. It describes how to live Zen.

Katsuki Sekida

Like Shunryu Suzuki, Katsuki Sekida (1903-1987), was born in Japan and spent most of his life there. But from 1963 to 1970 he taught Zen at the Honolulu Zendo and the Maui Zendo in Hawaii. While there he wrote numerous articles on Zen. Ultimately those articles were assembled and included in his book, *Zen Training.* Published in 1975, the book provides invaluable and in-depth insight into the practice of meditation.

R.H. Blyth

The Englishman, R.H. Blyth (1898-1964), actually went to the East to study the Ways of the East. After having lived in Korea from 1925 to 1935 he moved to Japan in 1936 where he lived until his death in 1964. In Japan he made a study of Zen and Japanese literature, while he maintained his Christian and Western beliefs and ways. He published much about Japanese literature and poetry, which got a lot of Americans interested in studying and living Zen. Because his explanations and interpretations of Zen were delivered from a Westerner's perspective, many Westerners were more easily able to relate.

Alan W. Watts

Born and educated in England, Alan W. Watts (1915-1973), moved to California in 1951 where he joined the faculty of the American Academy of Asian Studies in San Francisco. In 1957 he published the *Way of Zen*, one of the first bestselling books on Zen Buddhism. In the book he tries to demystify Zen for the Western mind. He does a particularly good job of it through, among other things, explaining the difference between Eastern and Western social convention and the thought process behind each. Ultimately, Watts wrote more than 25 books and articles on subjects important to Eastern and Western religion and philosophy.

Jack Kerouac

Jack Kerouac (1922-1969), one of the figureheads of the Beat Generation, embraced Buddhism as a way to fully realize life. Kerouac said the Beat Generation was a religious generation and described himself as a "strange solitary crazy Catholic mystic." His autobiographical novels, however, depict his fascination with Buddhism and trying to get his mind around Zen. But Kerouac and the novels he wrote, particularly *Dharma Bums*, helped to bring Zen to the forefront of what was the beginning of a cultural revolution in America.

Robert M. Pirsig

Robert M. Pirsig was born in Minneapolis, Minnesota in 1928. His book, *Zen and the Art of Motorcycle Maintenance,* published in 1974, is an autobiographical motorcycle journey from Minnesota to San Francisco with his 12 year old son that sold more than five million copies

Pirsig tells his story through

the use of Zen and Western psychology concurrently. This approach made it made the Zen seemingly less foreign and more acceptable to the Western reader.

ENLIGHTENMENT

"If you are unable to find the truth right where you are, where else do you expect to find it?" - Dogen Sengi

Enlightenment (nirvana in Sanskrit and *satori* or *kensho* in Japanese) is total realization of our true nature and our oneness with everything; that while we are each an individual we are at the same time all one, that duality or separation is an illusion of the ego and that the present moment is the only reality. To make enlightenment a goal, however, is wrong. There are no goals in Zen. To make enlightenment a goal is to never experience it. And having it, one would never think about wanting it.

Enlightenment is attained when we are able to free ourselves from all grasping and desire once and for all. It cannot be achieved by an intellectual understanding of what it is, as Bodhidharma indicated, but only through individual experience and an intuitive comprehension and oneness with the Truth as realized by the Buddha. The Truth is already inside each of us; it is our unity with all things. Zen cannot show you the Truth inside you, but it can point the way to it.

There are two ways of realizing enlightenment. One is through a gradual step by step advance towards it. This is the typical method and is sometimes referred to as "ladder Zen." This method is classically illustrated in the 10 pictures titled *In Search of the Missing Ox.* In Zen tradition the ox is associated with one's own true nature. The search for the ox represents the journey to find our true nature or inner Being. There are a number of versions but they all illustrate the same process. The 10 stages are listed here:

1. Begin the Search for the Ox
2. Discovering the Footprints
3. Catching Sight of the Ox
4. Catching the Ox

5. Taming the Ox

6. Riding the Ox Home

7. Ox Transcended, Self Remains

8. Ox and Self Transcended

9. Returning to the Source

10. Return to the World

The second way of realizing the Truth is called sudden and direct enlightenment. It may happen to someone who one day explodes with genuine enlightenment and undergoes an exhaustive and profound experience all at once. It is said that, almost as a boy, the sixth Patriarch, Hui-neng, achieved enlightenment this way upon hearing someone recite the Diamond Sutra. The Diamond Sutra, a Buddhist scripture, is one of Buddha's teachings, which elaborates on the diamond-hard edge of emptiness that can finally cut through delusion, leading to enlightenment.

Sudden and direct enlightenment has also happened to people with perpetual anxiety, or who have suffered a massive and traumatic loss or depression in their life, which has ultimately triggered within them a profound, spontaneous awakening to the Truth.

MEDITATION

"Nothing divides one so much as thought."
- R.H. Blyth

Most Zen practitioners arrive at their awakening through what is occasionally called "ladder" Zen, and the majority of those through the Soto school preferred method of *zazen.* There are, of course, other means of meditating besides sitting meditation, but none have been found to be as effective. For example, the Rinzai school believes that working with *koans* - reciting seemingly nonsensical antidotes - is effective preparation for a student's enlightenment.

Without question, however, the focus of traditional Zen practice is zazen. It is the surest way of developing the discipline necessary to realize one's true nature, of being mindful, and of maintaining a Zen lifestyle.

Through the practice of zazen we are able to quiet the mind and adjust our nervous activity. It is the ego, or second mind, that over time has come to dominate our decision making. We discriminate. We make decisions based on the belief that we are who we are as a result of our past, of what we do and how we are perceived by others. The ego would have us believe that we are each only an individual who must control every situation and prevail, regardless of the cost. This is the "illusion" – for the reality is that we are our inner Being, separate from our mind and body. But upon enlightenment our true nature becomes evident and we are exposed to the unity of all things.

In Zen the concept of "no mind" - in Japanese *mushin; mu* meaning no and *shin* meaning mind - means "no ego." No mind is essentially the same as our original mind, without the discriminating ego. The original mind is spontaneous and does not second guess. It makes decisions based on our awareness of the present moment.

This state of mind can be achieved by losing our self, as Dogen Zenji said, meaning to lose our ego. This allows us to realize our true nature which manifests compassion. This is done by living in the present moment and by nonattachment to our notions, ideas and concepts and by simply letting go. We let go by accepting that we have no control over anything or anyone other than ourselves. Negative thoughts will continue to enter the mind, but practicing zazen will show how to acknowledge each as it comes and then to release it and let it go. When you stop and recognize the workings of the ego, you do so with your original mind. It is as though you are observing yourself from outside yourself. Through this observation you experience a moment of enlightenment, or *kensho*, and are on the right path.

Posture

Typically we sit on the floor in zazen with some form cushion under the buttocks. It is important to remain stable and motionless for the duration of zazen. It also helps to wear clothing that is loose and does not bind.

It may be difficult to sit on the floor comfortably. Sitting in a chair is acceptable as long as we hold the correct posture.

The full-lotus position is the most common position when sitting on the floor during zazen; that is, with the right foot on the left thigh and the left foot on the right thigh.

The hands rest in the lap, one hand under the other, palms up and thumbs touching at the tips (the cosmic mudra).

There are other positons besides the full-lotus position. The important thing is for everyone to find what they are comfortable with and also allows for the best way to attain proper breathing.

When zazen is done while sitting in a chair, it is best that the chair has no arms to contact the elbows and interfere with concentration. Using a chair, one may cross the ankles and maintain a hand position in the lap similar to one used with the full-lotus position. The upper body position should be the same as that of the full-lotus position.

For all positions, the pelvis must remain stable while the waist muscles hold the upper body continually upright. With this proper posture the weight of the body will be concentrated in the lower abdomen. Tilt the head down just a bit and relax the shoulders and chest. Now take a deep breath, hold it for a moment and exhale completely.

Finally, stay calm, and without movement begin breathing correctly to move into deep concentration (*Samadhi* in Japanese).

Breathing

Breathing is a very important aspect of zazen and requires a good amount of effort. The focus on breathing helps preclude the random thought from entering the mind. Although periodic lapses of concentration will occur through renewed focus on breathing they can be dismissed.

Zazen breathing is different from normal breathing. The focus, or concentration, of breathing in zazen is on the lower abdomen. It is important to breathe slowly and rhythmically. When concentration is focused on the lower abdomen to maintain breathing thoughts do not sneak in. When exhaling, the breath should almost stop as it is slowly squeezed out by continual slow pressure of the diaphragm. Try to ensure continued tension on the lower abdomen during the entire process.

Beginners often start their meditation by counting their breath. Counting the breath helps to maintain concentration. And although it isn't really meditating, it will ultimately help with the discipline required to achieve the proper breathing required for zazen. There are three ways to count the breath. With each count only to ten and then begin again, visualizing the numbers as you count.

1. Count each inhalation only, skipping the exhalations until ten is reached.

2. Count each exhalation only, skipping the inhalations until ten is reached.

3. Count each inhalation and exhalation

as one until ten is reached and then begin again – that is, inhale and count "one," exhale and count "two," etc.

Even counting the breath will not keep thoughts from slipping into the mind. When they do, simply acknowledge them and then let them pass. Better concentration will increase with time.

During the breathing process just monitor the breath as it goes in and out. Don't be critical of yourself if is not going well or praise yourself if you think you are doing great. Both of those are forms of attachment and neither is Zen-like. Just follow the breath without comment or judgement.

Samadhi

With the proper posture and breathing in sitting meditation one may attain *Samadhi*, a state of meditative consciousness. In this state the mind becomes still and the activity of consciousness is stopped and there is no awareness of time, space or purpose.

This is a state of complete harmony and tranquility, coupled with a kind of alertness.

Emerging from *Samadhi* one may become completely aware of the One Body or one's own true nature. The Japanese word for this experience is *kensho* – *ken* meaning to see into something; *sho*, meaning one's true nature. *Kensho*, a momentary form of enlightenment or awakening, may be experienced from time to time.

Satori, a sudden and lasting enlightenment, is a Japanese word which means the realization of our true nature. One may experience their *satori* when coming out of absolute *Samadhi* in zazen or as mentioned, through other means not associated with sitting meditation.

Koans

A *koan* is a "Zen exercise" or "problem," originally based on anecdotes of past Zen masters.

The use of the *koan* method was developed by the Rinzai School of Zen and dates from the early twelfth-century in China. The *koan* method was used as a means of authorizing the advancement of "students" through the approval of someone - teacher or master - who had been previously approved. So, solving a *koan*, which the student is required to do intuitively, was similar to "passing" a test as a means of helping to validate one's *satori* prior to being able to claim a position of authority in the Zen tradition.

The process was intended to prepare the student or practitioner for enlightenment by realizing the true nature of all things. Zen believes in nonattachment and stresses avoidance of dualistic thinking. *Koans* are meant to be considered until they are internalized and comprehended on a level beyond reasoning and logic. Although a spontaneous response is ideal, it may take days, months or longer before the right answer is given, either verbally or by way of a nonverbal demonstration.

Not everyone appreciates *koans*.

Some Zen practitioners find little value in trying to unearth a correct answer to a seemingly illogical question. But for others *koans* help center the mind, and intuitively understanding them does bring them closer to their awareness of the oneness of all things.

Zen teaches that nothing is really within our control other than our selves. Plans are made and something happens at the last minute and everything changes. Is this a "bad" thing? No, it just is. Because of this lack of control, from time to time life appears ridiculous or illogical. The world, the cosmos even the nature of things, are not charted out for our understanding. *Koans* are a means of absorbing this illogical logic and moving us to a place of simply being and doing. To just be and do is the essence of Zen.

To Westerners, koans may appear illogical to the point of lunacy. This feeling is reinforced by the inherent difference in the way people in the East and West have come to view the world we inhabit. Not that we live in different worlds, rather how it is perceived. For example, where someone from the West views the world as having been "made," which supposes influence by some external entity, someone from the East would more likely view it as having "grown," which supposes naturalness akin to Taoist thought. This dichotomy is reflected in our languages and analytical thinking and is significant.

Once understood and internalized, from this perspective the lesson of the *koan* is not lunacy or paradoxical but a step closer to realizing ones true nature.

As a result of our ego, or second mind, we have come to think in terms of duality. That is, an "I" and a "you," an "us" and a "them," "subject" and "object," "knower" and "known," "light" and "dark," etc. But is this reality true or is it an illusion, something temporary like the ripples in a pond – here one moment and gone the next. Where did they go? Were they ever actually there?

Although a *koan* may seem absurd,

it should be remembered that the point of practicing a *koan* is to expand one's awareness of the Truth. The following well known *koan* that at first may appear ridiculous was attributed to Master Tozan Ryokai:

A student once asked Tozan, "How can a person escape the cold and the heat?"

Tozan said, "Go to the place where it is neither cold nor hot.

"Where is such a place," asked the student.

Tozan said, "When cold, be cold. When hot, be hot."

Eventually the student could realize that the Master wanted him to really feel the heat without attaching to it. Not to look for reasons for not liking the heat and then dwelling on them, which is attachment and is what causes suffering. Just be hot. Really feel the heat - become the heat. That is the place where there is no suffering. But this does not imply merely submitting to the inevitable, for in Zen we are not a helpless pawn of circumstances.

The duality of the knower and known is as relative, as dependent on one another or mutual, as everything else. This is what the student must internalize and understand intuitively before he or she can advance their awareness of their own true nature. When there is no duality the suffering will cease with a flash of *kensho*.

Another famous *koan* again questions duality and the discrimination between things. It also demonstrates the spontaneous nonverbal response desired in solving the problem at hand.

Master Po-chang needed the right person to be the master of a new monastery he was going to open. So he gathered all of his students around and set a pitcher in front of them and said:

"Without calling it by its name, tell me what it is.

The top student spoke up, saying, "You could not call it a piece of wood."

At this point the monastery cook came in, kicked the pitcher over, breaking it, and walked away.

Po-chang immediately put the cook in charge of the new monastery for his correct response to the question.

The cook was living in Zen with no dualism and no discrimination. This *koan* addresses the issue of naming or labeling things, which fosters the false belief of the difference or separateness of things. Although the pitcher was not a piece of wood that answer was wrong because it implied that the two are different things. When the cook kicked and broke the pitcher he was rejecting the idea of a pitcher by breaking the item in question. Pitcher, no pitcher, piece of wood, Po-chang or the cook; all appear different but all may be as anything as well because nothing is really separate. They are one, not our ideas or notions of what they are.

There are scores of *koans*. A few more of the most well-known ones are: "What is Buddha?"; "What is the sound of one hand clapping?"; "Why did Bodhidharma come from the West?" and "Does a dog have Buddha Nature?"

Koans appear crazy or absurd because their purpose is to challenge the preconceived ways we view things by going beyond logic, intellect and our concept of duality.

LIVING ZEN

"Zen is not some kind of excitement, but concentration on our usual everyday routine." – Shunryu Suzuki

A Zen lifestyle means focusing on the present moment and taking our time so that whatever we are doing – standing, sitting, moving, resting, work or play – it is done perfectly and without hesitation. Zen clears our alertness by eliminating the past and future, and creates a harmony or oneness with the person and the task at hand. Alan Watts referred to it as "a state of unified or one-pointed awareness" in his book, *The Way of Zen.*

Today Zen is practiced by different people for different reasons: as a way to slow down and get in touch with one's self; for preventative medicine purposes due to its ability to relieve stress, which wears down the body through the release of hormones ultimately resulting in chronic diseases and loss of contentment; as a way of organizing one's personal and professional life, both physically and mentally; or to simply live life to the fullest without want or regret. Zen is not a philosophy or a religion but a psychology of liberating oneself from society's conventional thinking, and through which one may also experience enlightenment. In short, Zen is a way of life.

It is a hectic world out there and we get swept up in it every day. We have to stay connected! We need the latest smart phone, video game, computer watch, biofeedback wrist band, etc. We do everything through our phones or online: connect through the numerous social media sites, buy anything and everything, do our banking, pay our bills, text and instant message, listen to music, watch movies and TV shows. We watch the evening news and wonder how the world ever got to be the way it appears. At times it seems as if it's all spinning out of control. We rush to get the kids to school, ourselves to and from work and to meet our social commitments. We end up pulled in too many directions and with no end in sight the pressure builds and we begin to feel all alone. We wind up with feelings of frustration, anxiety, worry, fear, agitation and discomfort and all the other thoughts and feelings that sap our lives of the enjoyment they are meant to have.

Zen won't stop those feelings from coming, but it can help us slow down and deal with them so we may restore the composure and stability they deplete. After all, they are only our feelings, not who we are, and Zen shows us how to acknowledge them, feel and move through them and then let them go like a puff of cigar smoke. That alone is worth the effort. Like washing the windows of your house after years of accumulated build-up, Zen can clear the mind and enable us to view the world and live the experience-whole rather than the whole-experience. And it all starts by giving up the need for control.

Zen's approach to getting in touch with our inner Being, or true nature, is by doing so as directly as possible without external aids. Reading books about Zen or studying the teachings of the Buddha or working with a Zen teacher can act as a guide pointing the way, but realizing one's True nature must be done internally and intuitively.

Zen teaches that while we are all individuals we are also one with the universe and as such we are all the same. It says that the universe is natural and spontaneous and perfect as it is, just as we all are. But over time we have become deluded by our ego and have lost sight of our true nature, so we agonize over the past and worry about the future. The ego would have us believe that our thoughts and our feelings are who we are, that we are the product of our past actions. But we are not the product of our past actions and when we engage our thoughts and feelings we suffer. If, on the other hand, we merely recognize those thoughts or feelings, allow ourselves to really feel them and then let them go, we are living right where we should, in the present, and we do not suffer.

We have lost sight of our naturalness and of spontaneity and who we really are. That is where Zen comes in. It offers all of us regardless of race, religion, creed or country of origin, a way to again find our true nature that is within each of us by living in the present moment – the Eternal Now. By just being and doing!

Zen teaches that the world is complex and dynamic and ultimately not within our control. But over time we humans, with our superior brains, have come to think that we *can* control things. So our ego, or second mind, has a lot of trouble accepting it when things don't go our way. This is because we have come to confuse our inner self with our outer form and with our ego, which wants to be in control. Instead of being present the ego will continue to think and rethink about something that occurred in the past. We carry on internal dialogues with ourselves, giving credence to our thoughts and feelings based on something that does not exist, forming opinions and taking actions as a result of our perceived ability to control. Instead of stepping back, assessing a situation and moving on, we resist it and become anxious about things that were never really in our control. Likewise, we worry about the future, which never comes because there is only ever the present moment.

When the ego is involved with psychological time and trying to control a situation it becomes the source of our suffering. Zen exposes the ego for the illusion that it is and shows us how we can give up control and gain peace of mind. Not control over ourselves, just the attempt at trying to control everything else.

We are always thinking, and that is a good thing because it helps bring order to our lives. But when we engage our thoughts and emotions we suffer, are not present, and our inner Being continues to elude us. Practicing a Zen lifestyle and being mindful will anchor us to the present moment and allow us to fully appreciate life. To do so, however, we must continue to work at it.

We are not what we look like or what we do for a living. We are not how fast we run or how much money we make. These things change, as do all things. The only constant is our true nature, our oneness with all things. Zen master Dogen Zenji expressed this relationship of time when he suggested that firewood does not become ashes and that life does not become death, as the winter does not become the spring. He said that each moment of time is "self-contained and quiescent." To believe otherwise is delusional.

Through Zen we realize our own true nature and with it our love of all things. With that enlightenment we live every moment of our life right here right now, in the present. This is the truth that never changes.

METTA BUDDHA

"Love can be found anywhere, even in a guitar." - Bob 'the Bear' Hite

As young people on the cusp of adulthood we begin to envision our futures. We are not exactly sure how the world works, but at the same time our aspirations are high. We want to know how to achieve in life and what is the best way of doing so. We want to know who we are and how we are going to fit in.

At this point in life some of us will take up technical jobs while others will pursue higher education. Once so engaged or equipped we set out to take the world by storm. Our goal at this point is to improve an imperfect world we are certain only we now know how to do.

As the pursuit begins, however, we typically encounter a system resistant to change, expeditious or otherwise, and we begin to question even the best of our intentions. As we continue to perform in this atmosphere our work begins to be performed purely by rote. We begin to feel as though something is missing. We question the system and our place in it. We now ask the same question every previous generation has asked: "What is it all about? What is the meaning of our life here on this planet earth?" At this point we may seek answers to our questions in religion, or find ourselves in a quagmire of existential angst.

Oddly enough, we already have the answer. It has been with us all along, even though most of us do not see it. The meaning of life is so simple. We feel it, yet we resist it even as we call it by name. The answer is love. The Buddha's fundamental principal; *metta* – "loving kindness." But even as we are told this it fails to register with us.

We say that we seek love, look for it and strive for it. We say that we need love but that it hurts and causes us pain. Zen teaches us that we are deluded by our desire, attachment and dualistic thinking, which causes our suffering. The practice of zazen, nonattachment and mindfulness releases us from our suffering by allowing us to let go. In doing so we are able to discover our true nature, which we have had all along. Once in touch with our Being we find love everywhere and in everything. Then, as in the tenth stage of *Searching for the Ox* we return to the world without delusion and spread love everywhere we go.

CIGAR PRIMER

INSIDE CIGARS

Cigars   119

Cigar History   121

Cigar Tobacco   137

Building a Cigar   150

Smoking Cigars   165

Accessories   176

CIGARS

*"The most futile and disastrous day seems
well spent when it is reviewed through the
blue, fragrant smoke of a Havana cigar."*
– Evelyn Waugh

What can be said about a cigar that has not already been said or written? Since their discovery by the New World more than five hundred years ago, cigars have been glorified, dignified, vilified, and satirized; politicized, codified, objectified and sanctified; theorized, categorized and monetized! All over of a few leaves of rolled-up dried tobacco. But then people being people never do seem to take a unified position on much of anything. Although it is interesting, since any experienced cigar smoker will tell you that they smoke cigars for the calming effect they provide both mind and body during the act of smoking. The fact is a premium hand rolled cigar is a true work of art, grown and assembled by artisans for the pleasure of about an hour's worth of personal relaxation.

This being said, excessive smoking of premium stogies is not suggested or recommended. As with anything else, moderation is the key, whether alone or with others, such as during a Zen Cigar Sesshin. For one who appreciates a good cigar and is also a practitioner of Zen, what could be more pleasing and beneficial than to enjoy a fine cigar while exploring the means of containing our nervous energy on an ongoing basis with like-minded folks?

Understandably, from time to time someone with limited experience regarding the art of cigar smoking may be invited to attend a Zen Cigar Sesshin. It is for that reason that this primer has been included herein. It is intended to provide such a person with a brief yet decent knowledge of cigars in order to help make their attendance as rewarding and meaningful as possible.

CIGAR HISTORY

*"They had no good cigars there, my Lord;
and I left the place in disgust."*
- Alfred Lord Tennyson

The tobacco plant was brought to the Antilles by Aborigines from South America between 3000 and 2000 B.C. To those natives and their descendants, the tobacco plant was considered a spiritual source for their medicine and was used in ceremonies as well as for political and religious purposes. Tobacco was integral to their culture and overall way of life. To this day, in certain parts of the islands, it is used by the indigenous people for medicinal and ceremonial purposes.

In 1492 Christopher Columbus arrived at what today is known as Cuba. It was there among the verdant Cuban hillside that a search party sent ashore by Columbus encountered the locals smoking what is considered the prototype of the modern day cigar. Certainly they could not be considered premium smokes by today's standards, as they were no more than twisted leaves of uncured tobacco bound by corn husks. And their size, by comparison, would make today's Churchills look petite.

The Mayans also smoked tobacco fashioned as what could be considered cigars – twisted leaves of tobacco tied with twine. Mayan artifacts discovered in the Yucatan area of Mexico, dating from around the tenth-century, clearly demonstrate this. The word cigar itself, some believe, is the Spanish derivative of the Mayan word "sikar" which meant to smoke tobacco. Others believe the word comes from the word "cigarra," which is Spanish for cicada, due to its similar shape.

In any event, Columbus brought back samples of his new find when he returned to Spain. It didn't take long before the discovery of tobacco and its manifestation as the cigar became popular in Spain; primarily with the Spanish elite. Oddly, the Spanish government did not see fit to share their discovery of tobacco with the rest of the world and the manufacture and smoking of cigars was virtually confined to Spain for the next few hundred years. In 1731 the Spanish government actually created an organization called the Royal Manufacturers of Seville to further control the production and distribution of their prized cigars.

Notwithstanding Spain's grip on the tobacco trade, by the mid seventeen-hundreds Dutch traders had managed to bring cigars to Holland and then to Russia where they quickly grew in popularity.

But as a result of Britain's brief occupation of Cuba in the late 1700's, the British brought loads of Cuban tobacco back home and exposed it to the rest of Europe.

In 1803 another significant event occurred when Napoleon invaded Spain and his army experienced the pleasures of the coveted Cuban cigar. Following Spain's example, in just a little more than ten years after Napoleon's invasion, the French government had taken over the tobacco business in France and was manufacturing cigars for themselves.

As all of this was going on cigar production was starting up in a few other countries in Europe, and in 1810 America opened its first cigar factory. As larger segments of the world were introduced to Cuban "Habanos" and the convenience and popularity of cigar smoking grew, so did Cuba's cigar production. The tobacco growers continued to take over more farmland to meet the needs of an ever increasing demand. By 1855 tobacco was Cuba's largest cash crop and Cuba was exporting almost 400 million cigars per year. The major Cuban brands of the day were Romeo y Julieta, Punch and Partagas, all of which still exist today.

As a result of the growing popularity of the high quality Cuban brands, they began being knocked-off in bulk. To address the issue Cuba established the Havana Cigar Brands Association in 1870.

About this same time some countries in Europe increased their own cigar production to maximize that revenue source. By 1875, France alone was selling almost a billion cigars a year.

Back then America was making cigars on a limited basis; but now bigger and better cigar factories began being built. American grown tobacco accounted for the majority of the U.S. cigars then, but there was no comparison between the quality of American and Cuban cigars. That changed not long after the Civil War with improvement in the methods of tobacco production, with the premier growing areas now located in Florida, Pennsylvania, Ohio, New York and Connecticut. While most all other states had been growing crops of indigenous American tobacco, Cuban tobacco was introduced to Connecticut in 1762. Although their attempts failed to match Havana quality using Connecticut-grown Cuban seed tobacco, ultimately they did provide the industry with the Connecticut shade wrapper, recognized as one of the finest wrappers ever grown. Unfortunately, today virtually no Connecticut shade wrapper is being grown in Connecticut. In 2011 there were 700 acres planted for shade wrapper and in 2019 only about 140 acres, an 80 percent decline. The primary reason for the reduction in shade tobacco is competition from other regions of the world. Tobacco growers in Ecuador and Nicaragua are growing and selling what is termed "Connecticut seed" tobacco and paying considerably less to produce it. Another reason is the high demand for the commercial development of the growing land in Connecticut.

As the manufacture of cigars was becoming a significant industry in America, it was aided by an influx of skilled immigrant workers during the Cuban Revolution (1895-1898) who had worked in the Cuban cigar factories. At the time, America and Cuba were the largest producers of premium handmade cigars. Moreover, most of those produced in America were made with imported Cuban tobacco. By the turn of the century there were more than seven thousand cigar factories in America, with almost ten percent of those located in South Florida because of its close proximity to Cuba.

This was also the time of Queen Victoria's reign in Great Britain. The imposition of her straight laced views upon her subjects put a damper on many things during the Victorian era, not the least of which was her outlaw of the use of tobacco. Her influence was felt in America as well with the imposition of smoking bans similar to those in England. It was not until her son, Edward, Prince of Wales, ascended the throne in 1901 as King Edward VII that the ban was lifted with the utterance of his now famous line, "Gentlemen, you may smoke." Still, smoking bans have come and gone and come again through the years, some having a significant effect on cigar smoking. Curiously, as a result of the Surgeon General's original pronouncement of the ills of the use of cigarettes on January 11, 1964, there was a spike in cigar smoking, as it was viewed as an acceptable alternative to cigarettes.

The years following the end of World War I saw a decline in cigar smoking in the

Unites States. Cuban cigars had become pricey and although America had the ability to produce enough cigars for its own consumption, the more economical machine-made cigarette had become very popular. In an effort to compete, some cigar manufactures began making cigars by machine. Fortunately the quality of the smoke remained the same, since Cuban tobacco was still being imported and used in the cigar making process.

Eventually America's manufacture of machine-made cigars took its toll on the import of the more expensive Havana cigars. Cuba was dealt an even greater blow when its export of cigars to England precipitously dropped during World War II. This was as much a problem for English cigar smokers at the time as it was for Cuban cigar makers.

England's remedy for this problem was to obtain their premium quality cigars from the burgeoning Jamaican cigar industry. Jamaica had been growing tobacco commercially and producing quality cigars for about one hundred years; now, thanks to World War II and England's insatiable desire for high quality humidified cigars Jamaican cigars came into their own.

The cigars manufactured and sold in America saw a number of changes in the years following World War II. Within the first few years following the war, the price of cigars incrementally escalated some thee hundred percent. Manufacturing changes also took place with the use of homogenized tobacco leaves used for both binder and wrapper to mitigate the rising costs. In response, Cuba followed suit with its own completely machine-made cigars. This move cut the price of a good Cuban to half the cost of its hand-rolled counterpart. Every working stiff in America could now afford to smoke superior Cuban-made cigars.

Sadly, for lovers of a good Cuban cigar, these times did not last long. Shortly after the communist insurgent, when Fidel Castro came to power with the overthrow of the Fulgencio Batista regime in 1961, things abruptly changed. In 1962 President John F. Kennedy declared an embargo on all Cuban imported goods. But as they say, timing is everything, and just hours before his declaration, President Kennedy directed his press secretary, Pierre Salinger, to buy him one thousand H. Upmann Petit Coronas. Salinger did even better and obtained 1,200 of his boss's favorite smokes for him.

The use of Cuban tobacco was substantially reduced with the embargo. Now the American aficionado was faced with finding a suitable replacement. Initially it was the Canary Islands just off the northwest coast of Africa that filled the bill. As Spanish provinces, the Canary Islands had been manufacturing cigars since the 1500s. Although no tobacco was grown there due to the poor quality of the soil, its import there had been routine for hundreds of years. The Canary Islands were one of the first places to which experienced Cuban cigar workers fled to escape Castro's new communist regime. With an abundant supply of quality tobacco coming in from the Dominican Republic, Jamaica and Honduras, the Canary Islands soon became America's number one supplier of premium hand-made cigars. This also gave rise to the creation of new brands, as well as the start-up of brands made there that were also being made in Cuba.

As cigar makers were ramping up production of brands new to the Canary Islands, still others, disenchanted with Castro's nationalization of all things Cuban, began to look for different suitable locations in and around the Caribbean Sea for their new home. The first and most obvious choice was Jamaica. It had existing factories, a skilled cigar making work force and quality tobacco could be grown on the island.

The Dominican Republic was also viewed as a Cuban rival for the same reasons as Jamaica with a notable exception - the island's Ciabo Valley. This area arguably has some of the best soil for growing high quality tobacco outside of Cuba's Pina del

Rio growing area. While Cuban Havana's are still considered the gold standard by most today, without question, Dominican companies fabricating Dominican brands produce hand-rolled cigars of equal or better quality.

During the 1960s and 1970s, when Jamaica and the Dominican Republic were coming to prominence, two other countries in Central America were entering the world of cigar production with their own products. Spotty at first as a result of their political climates, Honduras and Nicaragua began producing cigars that were competitive in price and quality with the other producers. It is each one's different, yet quality soil for growing cigar tobacco that has allowed them to endure. All of these countries produce unique tasting cigars due to the differences in their soils, giving the knowledgeable cigar smoker an array of premier product from which to choose.

In hindsight the Cuban embargo actually turned out to be a blessing in disguise, not only for American premium cigar smokers, but for the cigar smoking world at large as well. At some point, the prime cigar tobacco growing areas of the Dominican Republic, Honduras and Nicaragua would likely have come into play. But the Cuban embargo forced the manufacturers' hands much sooner. With new and divergent growing areas came new brands and experimentation with new blends and styles that continue on today.

The zenith for premium cigar smoking and sales in the U.S. was 1964 with approximately nine billion cigars sold that year. A gradual decline in sales began a few years later in 1972 reaching a nadir of just slightly more than two billion premiums sold in 1996. A number of factors contributed to the decline, not the least of which was the Surgeon General's revised position that cigars were not an acceptable alternative to cigarette smoking, and the State of California's requirement in 1988 that cigar packaging include labels warning of health hazards. Today California residents are even required to listen to a warning before finalizing a purchase of cigars over the internet.

Outside of the U.S. the 1980s were also witness to shifts in cigar manufacturing due to a questionable move by the Cuban government. In 1989 its Cubatabaco came out with a new requirement that it must own fifty-one percent of any enterprise importing Cuban cigars. This was intended to ensure its fair share of profits; but what it did was effectively end cigar production for non-Cuban based companies. Other contributing factors were the conversion of some tobacco producing land to food production for the Cuban people and the occasional effect of hurricanes on tobacco growing and manufacturing.

Through the 1980s Cuba was exporting about ninety million premium cigars per year. By around 1995 that number had been reduced to about sixty million.

In a bold but savvy move, in 1994 the government-owned Cubatabaco privatized its marketing efforts by contracting with Habanos S.A. for the majority of its international sales efforts. As a result Cuban cigar sales have slowly rebounded to current sales in the neighborhood of just over one hundred million Havanas a year.

The remainder of the notable premium, hand-rolled cigars produced for world consumption come from the Dominican Republic, Honduras and Nicaragua and to a lesser degree from Mexico and Jamaica.

In 2016 there were an estimated sixteen million dedicated premium cigar smokers in the United States. In 2015, 3.7 billion large premium cigars were consumed in the U.S., or about sixty-five percent of the total global production of large premium cigars.

When those aficionados are asked why they smoke their cigars, the first reason usually given is that it is a way of relaxing that puts them in touch with themselves. The second reason is for the comradery. But if you smoke cigars you don't have to ask the question because you already know the answer.

CIGAR TOBACCO

"Tobacco may seem a rough, rank weed to some, but its nature is fragile and it demands a kind of brooding care."
- Jerome E. Brooks, *The Mighty Leaf*

Location, Location

Just as only certain regions around the globe produce the finest wines, there are only a handful of areas capable of producing the world's finest premium cigar tobacco. With few exceptions, all of those areas are in countries within or immediately adjacent to the Caribbean Sea. They are Cuba, the Dominican Republic, Honduras and Nicaragua.

Climate and soil are the reasons these areas can consistently grow the quality of tobacco – flavor, aroma, and burn – prized for use in the best quality cigars. The tobacco growing regions of these countries, each with their own particular characteristics, combined with the Caribbean climate of warm sunny days, clear nights and the right amount of rain, will produce a cigar with a personality all its own. This is the reason that a cigar produced in any one of these countries tastes different from one produced in any of the other countries.

Even if you were not aware of any other country from which cigars come, it is a pretty sure bet that you know they come from Cuba. Since the days of Columbus, Cuba has been producing the cigars by which all others are measured. The reason Cuban cigars stand out is due to the quality of the island's soil. Even among the island's four growing areas, the suitability of the soil for different types of leaves varies. The soil in the Vuelta Abajo region at the western end of the island is like no other, and grows tobacco for all three parts of a cigar; filler, binder and wrapper. Combined, these tobaccos are what define a "Havana" "*puro.*" ("Havana" because Cuban cigars became associated with the port city they were shipped from and "*puro*" - which is Spanish for "pure"

- because only a cigar made entirely from the tobacco of the same country of origin is called a *puro*). The Partido region, just east of the Vuelta Abajo, grows wrapper and filler only. Both the Remedios region in the center of the island and the Oriente region at the eastern side of the island grow only binder and filler.

Although there are a number of countries making cigars today, only three make cigars that can rival the quality of a premium Cuban cigar. This is due to the qualities of their own tobacco growing soil. Today the Dominican Republic produces the lion's share of the world's premium cigars and the soil of its Ciabo Valley is the best. It produces excellent binder and filler, but no leaf for wrapper. A second area is the *Real* region, which also produces binder and filler but no wrapper. Thus, Dominican cigar makers must import the wrappers for their quality cigars from other locations that specialize in producing wrappers, such as Sumatra, Ecuador, Cameroon, Mexico and Connecticut in the U.S., which is quickly dwindling.

Honduras, in Central America, is second only to the Dominican Republic in the production of non-Cuban premium cigars. Tobacco is grown in the La Entrada and Jagua valleys. Like other places in and around the Caribbean, the cigar industry in Honduras expanded in the 1960s when experienced cigar workers and manufacturers fled the Castro regime. Many of them brought Cuban tobacco seed with them to their new homes. But the resulting tobacco wasn't always the same. It depends on the character of the soil. That is why the Cuban seeds grown in Honduras produce a fuller bodied tobacco than those grown in the Dominican Republic, which is known for its milder tobacco.

Nicaraguan soil also has the capability of producing top notch premium cigars. There are three areas in the country with the right type of fertile, nutrient-rich soil for producing top grade filler, binder and wrapper. They are the Esteli and Valapa Valleys and the Condega region to the north. Unfortunately, over the years cigar production in Nicaragua had been somewhat hit and miss. Joya de Nicaragua cigars, for example, were good cigars in the 1970s and 1980s until production came to a halt due to political unrest. And although production resumed some years later, the brand is still not quite the same. Although today, many puros coming out of Nicaragua definitely rival anything from Cuba.

Seed, Sun & Shade

Seed, sun and shade are the trifecta for growing tobacco leaves. A commercial sun grown tobacco plant can reach a height of five and a half to six feet tall. A shade-grown plant will reach a height of between eight and ten feet tall. Each plant produces as many as one million seeds (enough to plant one hundred acres of tobacco). The seeds are tiny, each one no bigger than a granule of refined sugar. Each tobacco plant produces approximately twenty light to dark green leaves per plant. The leaves are oblong shaped and an average of twenty-seven inches long and seventeen inches wide, with pointy tips.

In and around the Caribbean the growing season begins in the late summer. The seeds are first placed in growing flats with individual sections - two or three seeds per section. The seedlings are shaded from the sun with cheese cloth and carefully maintained by attendants during this period. After a few weeks, the smaller seedlings will be removed from the flat's individual sections, leaving only the larger, strongest one. After the plants are about a month old, they grow rapidly until maturity. Within forty-five to sixty days the seedlings are transplanted to the large growing fields without the shade cover. They remain there until full maturity and ready for harvest, about forty to sixty days. Shade-grown tobacco in the field, however, is grown under a suspended canopy of cheese cloth or mesh.

While in the growing fields tobacco plants are subject not only to changes in weather patterns, but to disease and infestation as well. Where too much or too little rain can affect the length of the growing season, disease and infestation can destroy all or part of an entire crop.

Even with careful monitoring by the growers and the use of pesticides and fumigation, insects still manage to damage the tobacco plants. The most common pests are aphids, the tobacco hornworm and the tobacco beetle. Aphids cause damage to the plant by sucking the juice from the leaves. The tobacco hornworm is three to four inches long, green with white stripes on the sides and a reddish horn near the rear end. They lay their eggs on the leaves. They are insatiable eaters that can consume the leaves of an entire plant. Then there is the tobacco beetle. It lays its eggs in the tobacco leaf. The larvae then proceed to devour the tobacco leaves. Sometimes leaves will be processed with unhatched eggs in them, which can show up later in an under-humidified humidor. If they hatch they can ruin an entire box of cigars. Not a good thing!

Growers also have to be constantly vigilant for various diseases. Long periods of continuous rain, prolonged cold snaps, and reduced sunshine are the catalyst for diseases, such as the Mosaic Virus. It results in ruined tobacco leaves. Black Shank will destroy an entire plant from the inside out as it turns the whole length of the stalk black. And Blue Mold can devastate an entire season's crop. It starts on the underside of the leaves, ruining the leaf first and then the entire plant.

While still subject to potential threats, when the plants are ready for their first harvesting, or priming, of which there may be as many as six, leaves from the lowest third of the plant are taken because they mature first. These are known as *Volado* leaves and are the mildest on the tobacco plant. Leaves on the top third of the plant remain on the longest and are known as *Ligero* leaves. The *Seco* leaves in the middle section of plant tend to be larger and are taken intermittently. They have great flavor and can be used in any part of a cigar. No more than three or four leaves are taken from any plant per priming. Removing the leaves from the stalk of a plant is normally done by hand and is difficult and time consuming labor.

Which section of the plant a leaf comes from will determine what part of a cigar it will become, depending on the maker's recipe. Seco leaves are used a great deal for wrappers in mild to medium bodied cigars because of their finer texture and abundant flavor. *Ligero* leaves, with the strongest taste and texture, may be used for wrapper in full bodied cigars and as binder in others due to their durability. Volado leaves from the lowest priming are typically blended with both top and middle leaves to create balanced filler.

As the leaves are harvested, they are separated by hand based on size, texture and condition. The leaves are then bound together at the base of the stem and taken to curing barns. Here the leaves are fixed to long poles that are hung up to allow the air to circulate around the leaves to remove moisture. Humidity and temperature are controlled in the curing barns where it takes about fifty days to sufficiently dry the tobacco leaves. During this period, the leaves gradually turn from green to a rich brown color.

Today there is a new high-tech curing method being used, known as Calfrisa. This state-of-the-art system is computer controlled and involves ductwork that runs along the roof and floor of the curing barn and continually maintains the perfect temperature and humidity. It is a far better method than the traditional vent heating system. It is expensive, though, and as such its use is not currently wide spread.

When the drying process is complete the leaves are brought down, inspected again and separated by size, quality and color. They are then shipped off for fermentation.

In preparation for fermentation, the leaves are sorted by type and the separate types are bound together in small groups called "hands." Each priming is fermented separately. The tobacco hands are placed on top of one another in large piles known as "bulks." Bulks are large and can be five feet high and weigh as much as three or four tons. Heat is generated in the center of the piles during the approximately forty-five day fermenting or "sweating" process. The bulks are turned four to eight times by placing the top hands at the bottom of the pile to maintain even heat during the process. The internal temperature of a bulk is allowed to range between 120 degrees and 160 degrees, depending on the type of tobacco being sweated. The heat during fermentation causes the tobacco's appearance and chemical makeup to change. The color becomes darker and the leaf more pliable as the minerals absorbed from the soil are purged and the high levels of ammonia nitrate, nicotine and tar are significantly reduced. Leaves intended for Maduro (Maduro is Spanish for mature) are sweated at higher temperatures and for longer periods of time. This converts more of the starch in the leaf to sugar, which results in a naturally sweeter taste.

When fermentation is complete, the hands are removed from the bulks and the leaves are carefully individually separated. Once again they are sorted by type, inspected and graded. Each leaf is then repackaged and categorized by place of origin, type and date. The packs of leaves are then sent to the manufacturers' warehouses for aging, typically for one to three years.

After aging, the leaves are taken out of storage and once again they are inspected, and then lightly moistened with a water mist. They are then hung to allow the any excess water to drain off. This "casing" process is done to make the leaves pliable to work with. Next the leaves are steamed and deveined and any broken leaves are pulled. They are inspected once more and now graded and sorted as binder, filler or wrapper. These three types of leaf are sent to the manufacturer for blending in accordance with a desired recipe. Ultimately each blend is unique and may use tobaccos of different ages, and from different countries of origin per a blender's particular brand. The tobaccos used and in what amounts will determine if a cigar is a mild, medium or full bodied smoke. Recipes are closely held secrets and a blend's consistent flavor, year over year, will help ensure customer loyalty to the brand.

BUILDING A CIGAR

"If you can't send money, send tobacco."
- George Washington

It is now time for the tobaccos to actually be brought together to construct a cigar. The process of building a quality handmade premium cigar involves numerous people, artists really, including those responsible for ongoing quality control. It begins with the selection of tobaccos to be used. A master blender is an artist with an intricate knowledge of all of the tobaccos available for creating signature premium cigars. His vision will define the taste, body style and appearance of a cigar. To create a premium handmade cigar, a blender will choose from hundreds, if not thousands, of varieties of tobacco that vary by country, region, seed and priming.

The filler of a premium cigar is long leaf tobacco from different primings.

Short filler - shorter chopped-up pieces - is usually what is used in a machine made cigar. Long filler produces a long ash, while short filler will produce a shorter ash, which tends to break apart before it can gain any length as it burns. Filler usually includes three types of tobacco selected for their robustness. Filler does not have to be visually appealing since it is not visible in the final product. While filler contributes only about thirty percent of the flavor of a cigar, it can account for virtually one hundred percent of the strength or body of a cigar.

Binder surrounds and holds the filler leaves together. The binder is usually somewhat neutral in flavor to compliment rather than compete with the filler and wrapper. In a premium cigar, the binder is made from a single whole tobacco leaf. It is selected for its structural strength and ability to burn continuously and evenly. As with filler, binder leaves do not need to be visually pleasing since they are not seen. Binder leaf contributes only about ten percent of a cigar's flavor, but is quite important in maintaining a cigars integrity and burn.

The wrapper is considered by many to be the most important part of the cigar. It is an indication of what is to come, and as such, it should invite rather than repel the potential smoker. Like curb appeal in selling a house, if the aesthetics are poor, what are we to think of the overall quality?

Wrappers vary in color, texture, age and aroma and account for as much as sixty percent of a cigar's flavor. A quality wrapper will be pleasing to the eye, free of blemishes, cracks, holes or stains. It should be well veined, but without ribs, and supple to the touch. It is for these reasons that quality wrapper leaves used in premium cigars are expensive and in chronic short supply.

The process for building a premium handmade cigar involves bunching and rolling entirely by hand as the term implies. A box will carry the *"Hecho en Cuba"* (Made in Cuba) *"Totalmente a Mano"* (made totally by hand) if made in Cuba, or Nicaragua if made there, etc. This sets them apart from hand-rolled and machine-made cigars. Machine bunched cigars have the bunch assembled by machine and the wrapper applied by hand. Manufacturers will make this distinction by stamping or printing "*Hecho a Mano*" (made by hand) on boxes of cigars made this way, or otherwise only partly hand finished. Cigars that are machine-made are put together totally by machine and will only carry the stamp "*Hecho en Cuba.*" Also, non-premium, mass produced machine-made stogies will use chopped tobacco as filler, a homogenized binder made of finely chopped tobacco bound by cellulose and either a whole leaf or homogenized wrapper.

Premium handmade cigars may, in certain instances, be made by a single "*tocedor*" or roller. But normally there are teams of two or even three people; a "buncher" and a roller or two bunchers and a roller. The buncher assembles the different leaves for the recipe, places them side by side, takes them in his hand then brings them together like an accordion.

This results in many continuous air channels that run the length of the cigar, which allows for an easy draw as the blend burns evenly.

If there are too many leaves in a bunch it won't draw. This is known as a "plugged" cigar and is the most common problem. If too few leaves are used a cigar will burn hot, as a result of too much air inside, and burn the tongue.

Another sign of a poorly made cigar is when it burns unevenly or down one side faster than the other. This occurs when the filler has been "booked." This happens when the leaves have been placed on top of each other and folded over to create a bunch. Along the fold it resembles the spine of a book, hence the term. This results in more tobacco on one side of the cigar, rather than an even distribution. Of course, booking, as well as too much or too little tobacco, is not a good thing.

The bunch is now placed on the binder leaf and the binder is rolled by hand around the bunch for placement in a wooden form. The form is the precise shape of the cigar the roller is making. Each such form generally holds ten bunches. When full, the forms are stacked on top of one another and placed in a bunch press. The press squeezes the bunches into their final shape. Bunches remain in the press for about an hour. They are rotated twice to eliminate creasing down the sides where the forms come together. When the partially completed cigars are removed from the bunch press, they are passed through a ring gauge to ensure the proper thickness of the cigar being made. Some makers also perform a draw test on each cigar at this point. Performed by hand, the head of each cigar is placed at the end of a mechanical vacuum tube which draws air through the cigar. The results are registered on a gauge. If the draw is not right, the partially completed cigar will be pulled.

Next, the roller places the partially finished cigar on a moistened wrapper leaf that he has cut to size for the cigar being rolled. Cigars are rolled with the outside of the wrapper leaf on the outside of the cigar because it is smoother than the veiny underside. Experienced rollers may get between twenty and thirty wrappers from a single leaf.

Finishing touches are now made to complete the cigar. The cap, a small circle of tobacco made from the remnants of the wrapper leaf to maintain uniform color, is affixed to the head of the cigar with a natural, tasteless gum. The stick is then trimmed at the foot to its proper length. The roller has now given the cigar its shape, size or ring gauge, and length, all based on the blender's recipe of filler, binder and wrapper. Cigar sizes are measured in length by inches. Thickness, or diameter, is measured by ring size, which is calibrated in increments of $1/64^{th}$ of an inch. So a 6"x64 cigar would be six inches long and one inch in diameter.

Back in the day, manufacturers provided readers, or *lector de tabaqueria*, for their workers as they did their job in the cigar factories. These people would sit or stand on a platform in front of the workers, like a teacher in front of a class, and read aloud to all of the artisans to keep their routine from getting to them during the long day. The material read would be mostly from classic literature and sometimes daily newspapers. Most factories dropped the readers when radio came on the scene early in the 20th century. Today it is a combination of radio and personal digital players that keep the monotony at bay.

As an interesting aside, Nilo Cruz's Pulitzer Prize-winning play, *Anna in the Tropics, is about a Cuban-American family in* Ybor City, Florida in 1929 awaiting the arrival of their new lector, Juan Julian, for their cigar factory. When he arrives, he begins reading from the Russian classic, *Anna Karenina*, and the scandalous lives of Tolstoy's characters start to intertwine with the lives of his listeners. The whole play takes place inside the factory. Members of the cast actually roll cigars on stage during the play and at one point smoke them. It is worth seeing if you get the chance.

The speed and level of ability at which an experienced *tocedor* performs can be amazing. They are proud of what they do and it shows in their work. The best are Zen-like in that they are mindful of what they are doing, yet become lost in the activity to the point that they become one with it. A highly experienced roller can make upwards of 500 cigars per day, depending on the size and type. However, conscientious makers' of premium cigars will limit their production to between 200 and 250 cigars per day to maintain quality. Larger cigars such as Churchills, and the more complicated shapes like Panatelas and Figurados, take more time and a good roller may complete no more than 80 to 100 of such cigars per day.

When a roller has finished a certain quantity of cigars they are bound together in bundles of fifty. Each bundle is labeled with the roller's name and the name of the inspector. This enables tracking of each roller's and inspector's performance, which is important for quality control.

Next the bundles are weighed to ensure that the proper amount of tobacco has been used. Bundles that are not within a tiny margin of error for the proper weight are sent back to the roller to be redone. Bundles are now undone and each cigar is passed through another ring gauge and given another visual inspection.

The next step in the process is to re-bundle the completed cigars and move them to the aging room. This is where the excess moisture the tobacco acquired to keep it pliable during rolling is removed. This is also when a blend's different tobaccos mingle and permeate one another in order to ultimately deliver a wonderful smoke. The cigars remain in these traditionally cedar lined, climate controlled areas for about a month. Some of a manufacturers' higher premium or vintage brands may remain in the aging room for four to six months or longer.

Cigars that are to be "box pressed," that is, given a rectangular or square shape, do not go straight to the aging room. They are taken and placed in wooden trays that hold about twenty five cigars. A cedar divider is hand placed between each cigar in the tray and a wood lid is then placed on the tray. The trays are then placed in a master press for four days at which point they are turned and replaced in the press for another four days. After the second four-day period, the box pressed cigars are removed from the trays and taken to the aging room.

When the cigars have been aged, they are taken from the aging room, separated by color and inspected. There are scores of color variations among wrappers but those in a single box must be uniform, as must those for a particular brand. Those that don't make it, end up being pulled and are either sold as seconds or are made into short filler. You never get a second chance to make a first impression! Quality makers know this and realize the importance of a cigar's aesthetics; a quality outside implies a quality inside.

After the cigars have been sorted by color and style, the bands are put on each cigar by hand - another time consuming task. The cigars are placed against a wooden guide with markings for the bands' locations to ensure they are applied at the exact same spot on each cigar. Originally bands were used to help keep the wrapper from unraveling during smoking. Due to advancements, that problem has been resolved. Today the purpose of the band is for identification of the cigar's brand and place of origin. Some accomplish this with a simple design, while others employ what would appear to be a miniature piece of fine art.

With the bands on the cigars they are now placed by hand inside individual cellophane wrappers, if it is the manufacturer's practice to do so. Some do, as the cellophane helps maintain the integrity of the cigars during transport, while others choose not to with the thought that the cigars will continue to age without encasement of any type (cellophane, glass or aluminum tube, or paper box). Many believe that cigars continue to age right up to the time they are smoked, and that the best way to aid the process is to remove the cellophane or other encasement before placing them in the humidor. This seems to have merit, as the longer a stick remains in the humidor – three months, six months or more – the mellower it is when smoked.

This is easily demonstrated. Take a cigar you like and age it for six months, then buy the same cigar and compare them. The one just purchased will usually be stronger in taste than the aged one.

The last step in the process is to give a final inspection to each individual cigar, then place the finished cigars in their boxes for shipping.

Before the introduction of the cigar box in the early 1800s, cigars were sold in bundles. And until recently, it used to be that, due to the Revenue Act of 1864 (as amended), each retail box had to contain a multiple of twenty-five cigars and a tax stamp to be sold legally.

Cigars inside the boxes were stacked in horizontal rows referred to as 8-9-8 due to alternating rows of eight on top, nine below, etc. on down to the bottom. Although this is still the norm, today many manufacturers have gone to ten-, twelve-, eighteen- and twenty-count boxes. The reason for this could be as simple as cost. There are a lot of "boutique" brands out there today making premium and super premium cigars that can be expensive. This is due to the higher quality tobacco, more expensive workers, zero tolerance for errors, aging time, etc. A box of twenty-five such cigars could be cost prohibitive for the average smoker. By reducing the number of cigars per box, one can still afford to purchase a whole box, as the price becomes more palatable. Notwithstanding the cachet of being able to purchase an entire box, doing so is cheaper overall than buying individual cigars.

The mass produced cardboard box aside, boxes for premium cigars are for the most part made by hand. There are generally two types: a cedar plywood box and an all-cedar or mahogany "cabinet box." Cabinet boxes have brass hinges and a brass clasp. Boxes are obviously another point of pride for cigar manufacturers. However, a box that is too fancy – made of mahogany, polished or beveled cedar, aluminum or leather bound – will not do much more than add to the cost of the contents.

Smoking Cigars

"Gentlemen, you may smoke."
– King Edward VII

When you go to a tobacco shop to purchase a good cigar and you ask the proprietor to tell you what they like, the savvy ones will tell you that what they like doesn't matter; it's what you like that counts. And, in fact, the best cigar is the one that you prefer. The experienced proprietor or sales person will then try to narrow your range of selection by determining your preference for a mild, medium or full bodied smoke; and from there to a shape, length and gauge with which you feel comfortable.

The best premium handmade cigars come from Cuba, the Dominican Republic, Nicaragua and Honduras. In general, Cuba is known for producing fuller bodied cigars; the Dominican Republic is associated with more mild cigars, and Honduras and

Nicaragua are known for their medium to full bodied smokes. To help define the strength of a cigar visually, one need only check the color of the wrapper. As a rule of thumb, the darker a wrapper's color, the fuller bodied the taste will be. The following are the seven separate basic wrapper colors:

Double Claro: Also referred to as Candela, this wrapper is very mild to sweet in flavor.

Claro: Also referred to as Natural, light brown in color with a very mild flavor.

Colorado Claro: Light reddish-brown and grown in direct sun, it is well matured.

Colorado: Dark reddish-brown. They have a rich flavor and subtle, pleasing aroma.

Colorado Maduro: A brown between Colorado and Maduro. Not much aroma.

Maduro: Between deep reddish-brown to virtually

black. It imparts full flavor and mild aroma with a
hint of sweetness.

Oscuro: Jet-black in color and
strong in flavor.

As with most things, cost will factor
into your purchase. All things being equal,
the cost of a premium handmade cigar
increases with the quality of the tobacco,
the amount used, and the length of time the
cigar was aged. Many brands are producing
"vintage" premiums today which cost
well more than a good premium, such as:
Series V Melanio by Oliva; the Aniversario
series by Padron; the Family Reserve series
by Padron; and the Estate Sun Grown by
Ashton. While those mentioned here are
excellent cigars, there are also expensive
cigars that are simply overpriced. Your
favorite need not come with an extravagant
price tag.

One evening on the *Tonight Show*,
Jay Leno, while interviewing George Burns,
noted that Burns made good money and
therefore must smoke expensive cigars.

Burns held up his cigar and responded by saying that he actually smoked the cheapest cigars he could find. Pointing to the holder on his cigar, Burns told Leno that when you use a holder, all cigars taste the same. Certainly not why most aficionados smoke premiums, but he made his point.

Aware of where the best handmade premium cigars come from, our strength or flavor preference, and what factors into the cost, we now need to determine a shape and size we prefer.

The same cigar shape may differ in size from one brand to another. As previously noted, size is determined by two things: length and ring gauge, or diameter. The size of a cigar does not, however, determine its strength. That is determined by the tobacco used. Although, a longer larger ring gauge cigar will produce a greater amount of smoke and will burn slower and cooler than a thinner shorter one. Also, there should be no expectation that a shape from one brand will taste anything like the same shape from a different brand.

When it comes to shapes most premium cigars are straight-sided and are either round or box pressed, with a closed head that requires clipping and an open foot for lighting. The standard shapes are as follows:

Petit Corona: 4½ inches with a ring gauge of 40 to 42. Essentially a miniature Corona

Corona: 5½ to 6 inches with a ring gauge of 42 to 44.

Corona Gorda: 5⅝ inches with a ring gauge of 46.

Toro: 6 inches with a ring gauge of 54 to 60.

Double Corona: 7½ to 8½ inches with a ring gauge of 49 to 52.

Churchill: 7 inches with a ring gauge of 47.

Robusto: 4¾ to 5½ inches with a ring gauge of 48 to 52.

Panatela: 5 to 7½ inches with a ring gauge of 34 to 38.

Lonsdale: 6½ inches with a ring gauge of 42.

Pyramid: 6 to 7 inches with a ring gauge of 40 at the head, widening to 52 to 54 at the foot.

Belicoso: 5 to 6 inches with a ring gauge of 50. Originally a short Pyramid, however many today are like Coronas with a tapered head.

Perfecto: Anywhere from 4½ to 9 inches, with a ring gauge of 38 to 48. It has a closed foot and rounded head.

Culebra: The Culebra ("culebra" is Spanish for snake) is three cigars braided together tied with a string. The three are separated and smoked individually. A typical Culebra is 5 to 6 inches long with a 38 ring gauge.

Some things remain constant among the selection of any premium cigar. First would be the overall appearance or aesthetics of the cigar. It should be uniform in appearance, both in color and contour. There should be no blemishes, bumps, holes or stains visible on the wrapper, nor should it be too veiny. A slight oiliness to the wrapper indicates proper curing. From a tactile standpoint, it should be firm to the touch, yet pliable when light pressure is applied with the fingers. It should have an alluring bouquet for the nose, which will mean a pleasant aroma as it burns. The cap should be affixed firmly to the head and there should be no "stems" visible in the tobacco at the foot of the cigar. All of these things imply quality construction and care on the part of the manufacturer.

When you select a cigar that meets these criteria you are fairly certain of a good smoke. Yet, one cigar does not a good brand make. Even with all of the quality control that is part of producing a first rate premium cigar, there are typically one or two per box, even from the brands known for their quality, that will have problems. After all, they are made by human hands. And given the speed at which they are constructed, it is understandable. The main reason for this is that the cigars are sorted by color before being boxed. While all of the cigars in one box look identical – part of their allure – this does not mean that all of the cigars in the box were made by the same roller. So cigars made by less experienced rollers can end up in boxes alongside those of more seasoned rollers if the wrappers match. Less experience, of course, means a potential for more mistakes.

So, when we know what we are comfortable smoking, we then look for the primary factor for determining a good cigar, which is consistency. If a premium handmade cigar's quality of tobacco and quality of construction are not consistently the same, it cannot be considered a "good" cigar. The only way to be sure that a particular brand will be consistently good, regardless of price, is to buy and smoke an entire box. If the overwhelming majority of smokes in the box are indeed of the same quality, then you know you have found a good cigar. Of course, even good cigars from the same box will taste differently when smoked at different times of the day, before or after a meal, and with or without a cocktail. Even the location where the smoking occurs, and with whom, will play a part in the experience.

It is time to put flame to foot and light your premium cigar. But before you do, take a moment to appreciate all that has gone into producing and getting that small work of art into your hands.

Three years ago, at minimum, it began as a seed in a divot of soil in an indoor protected and nurturing environment. As a seedling, its progress was monitored ever so closely until it was ready to brave the days and nights of the balmy tropical climate on its own. Relocated to the open exposed growing fields, there it remained for months until harvested and sent off to be cured and fermented. Then off again to meet its maker who would combine and shape its adolescent parts in preparation for interment while it aged. Once matured, it is dressed, boxed and shipped off for your purchase and smoking pleasure. So before lighting that premium cigar, study it and appreciate the love that went into its making as you roll it between your fingertips. Close your eyes, inhale the bouquet and you can almost taste the tropical soil and sun.

When ready to light up, first clip the head. Be sure not to go below the cap or you risk the possibility of having the cigar unravel during smoking. Then hold it at a slight angle and touching it with the flame, char the foot. Now place the cigar in your mouth and hold the flame about an inch away from the foot as you slowly draw on the cigar while rotating it in your mouth. Be sure that it is completely lit so that it does not burn down unevenly. Once lit, some like to give it a quick blow to get any "impurities" out. The band is of no consequence, on or off, it is strictly individual preference.

Cigar smoke is not taken into the lungs. It is drawn into the mouth and held for a few moments then exhaled, providing flavor for the tongue and aroma for the nose.

How long a cigar is smoked depends on the individual smoking it. Some smoke only half the way down, as the tars and moisture increase at that point strengthening the taste. Others smoke it all the way to the end. It is a personal preference.

As of this writing, the record for the length of time for smoking a cigar is 3 hrs. 52 min. 55 sec. The record was set by Igor Kovacic at the 2019 Cigar Smoking World Championship held in Helsungbourg, Sweden. The cigar was a Macanudo Inspirado.

When done smoking a cigar, do not crush it out as though it were a cigarette. That would be unsightly and stinky. Merely set it down and leave it. It will go out without a smell in no time.

ACCESSORIES

"Open the old cigar-box, get me a Cuban stout," – Rudyard Kipling, *The Betrothed.*

Cutters

Because premium handmade humidified cigars are capped at the head, they must be cut in order to smoke them. There are three ways of achieving this: with a straight blade, with a 'V' cutter and with a punch. Each method employs a tool that can range anywhere in price from a few dollars to hundreds of dollars depending on who makes it, what it is made of and what nonessentials are added to it; such as engraving, inlay, gold plating, diamonds, etc.

First there is the guillotine cutter. There are a few variations but essentially all function in the same manner. The cigar's head is placed through a hole in the device and with a single fast action, either one or two sharp blades slices off the tip. This is the most functional cut as it provides the largest opening for conveyance of the greatest amount of smoke.

The 'V' cutter was developed for cigars with medium size ring gauges. The working end is relatively short and made of stainless steel. It has a hole at the end where the head of the cigar is placed. There is a thumb activated lever that has a V- like wedge with two razor-sharp edges, that when quickly pushed down slices a deep V in the cigar. As the cigar is smoked, tars and juices tend to collect at the location of the cut. V cutters come with either a long handle for tabletop use, or with a short handle for carrying in the pocket.

A punch, or bullet as it is sometimes called because it resembles one, is a hollow cylinder with a sharpened end that is inserted into the head of the cigar. When the punch is withdrawn, it removes the tobacco leaving a hole. The hole from a punch, being smaller than the area from a guillotine cut, provides less smoke and can concentrate tars and juices. Also, if inserted too deeply into the cigar, the punch can create a tunnel that will cause the cigar to burn hot.

Lighters

There are a number of items with which one may light a cigar, and again, a wide range in cost for those items.

If matches are used, wooden ones are better than paper or "book" matches. Wooden "box" matches are longer and produce a larger flame. Even so, they are not great on a windy day. You can also buy matches made specifically for lighting cigars. Longer than regular wood matches, they afford plenty of time to properly light any cigar. Similar, yet even better, would be to use strips of cedar called spills. They may be found in better tobacconist shops. You can also simply cut the cedar separator sheets that come in cigar boxes into thin strips for use as spills.

Many find lighters more convenient than matches. They come in many styles and sizes and can vary greatly in cost. There are basically two types of lighters: the fluid based lighter and the butane fueled lighter. The Zippo, for example, is a fluid lighter and usually not a first choice. Should the flame touch the cigar it can impart the taste of the petroleum based fluid, and it is not any better than a match on a windy day. The butane gas "jet" or "torch" lighters on the market today come in single, double or triple burner models. They are superb for effectively lighting any size of cigar. The flame burns clean and works well even in a strong wind.

Storage

To protect your valuables, you place them in a vault. To protect and preserve your cigars, you place them in a humidor. The purpose of a humidor is to replicate the tropical climate from which the cigars originate. The proper temperature is 70 degrees with a relative humidity of 72 percent. Minor fluctuations either way are acceptable. But wide swings can dry out or over-humidify your cigars. Too dry and they will lose the natural oils that create flavor, taste stale and burn hot. Over-humidified they will feel damp, be difficult to light and hard to smoke. Worse, they can wrinkle and even expand to the point of the wrapper bursting open. So regardless of style or size, a humidor is not worth having if it is not air tight and maintains the proper humidity.

Technically, a zip-lock plastic baggie with a damp paper towel inside is a humidor. But if used should be done on a limited basis. Anything that brings water into direct contact with a cigar wrapper should be avoided.

Most tabletop humidors are lined with Spanish cedar, which imparts a wonderful scent, but is also very absorbent. Before using it for the first time, a humidor needs to be "seasoned" or the cedar will draw all of the moisture from the cigars. To avoid this, the cedar is allowed to absorb the right amount of moisture by wiping the interior with a clean damp cloth, or by placing a damp sponge inside the humidor for a couple of days. Do not get the cedar too wet or it will warp and ruin your humidor. Either way, only use distilled water when seasoning your humidor, as well as for use in any humidifier. Tap water and bottled drinking water contain impurities that can contaminate your cigars. Today you can buy small, prepackaged humidifier bags to season as well as humidify your humidor. Depending on the size of your humidor it can take a few of them to do the job and replacements are required every few months. After seasoning, be sure to install a good humidifier and hygrometer and you should be good to go.

Finally, before purchasing a humidor, it is important to know your storage needs. A twenty-five count humidor will only hold twenty-five cigars of a certain size. It will thus accommodate fewer of a larger size. Be sure to check the dimensions before you buy to ensure it will hold plenty of your favorites.

ABOUT THE AUTHOR

J. F. Westbrook was born and raised in Los Angeles, CA. He studied architecture and urban planning in college. He is a former Peace Corps Volunteer and former Volunteers in Service to America (VISTA) Volunteer. Professionally he has worked as an urban planner, general contractor and real estate developer. He lives with his wife in Southern California.